Praise for *All of This*

"Unflinching and brutally precise. Wo[...]
barbaric accouterments of illness, and [...]
scenes like spikes. The barf bags and [...]
no-slip socks, the folding canes that [...]
walkers and then wheelchairs: It's a [...]
she nails it."
    —Meghan Daum, *New York Times Book Review*

"This isn't the typical book about grief and widowhood. While the title of the book comes from Hal's request that his wife write about 'all of this' (that is, his sickness and death), she admits it's unlikely that the finished product was what he had in mind. Rather, it's an unfiltered, unadulterated, uncouth, and often hilarious look at a marriage that was falling apart but was then upended by illness and death."
    —*The San Diego Union-Tribune*

"Disturbing and profound, this intimate book about one woman's path to personal liberation also reveals the sometimes-labyrinthine nature of the bonds that unite people in love. A provocative and memorable work of autobiography."
    —*Kirkus Reviews*

"Beautifully written, complex, provocative, painful, genuine . . . an unforgettable memoir."
    —Roxane Gay, bestselling author of *Bad Feminist*

"An authentic and profound book on the complexities of being human. Painfully beautiful, wonderfully lyrical, and uncomfortably honest in a way that is so rare, yet so needed."
    —Jenny Lawson, bestselling author of *Furiously Happy*

"Woolf takes readers on a journey that is nothing if not unforgettable. . . . [A] brutally honest and empowering tale of a woman who emerges from her marriage and her husband's final illness like a butterfly from a chrysalis—not neatly or painlessly, but nonetheless beautiful to behold. . . . Be prepared to laugh, to cry. . . . Readers will definitely be glad they got on this roller coaster with her."
    —*Library Journal*

"Aptly titled, *All of This* is an all-encompassing portrait of a marriage that didn't work, and Woolf is as unflinchingly honest about that marriage as she is about the experience of loss that terminated it."
　　—BookPage (starred review)

"*All of This* is a lot. Woolf is at her best when deep in the details, conjuring her experience onto the page with her rich command of imagery, metaphor, and symbol: 'the sun . . . cracking its egg over the muggy horizon,' the grape soda Hal craved and then rejected, her daughter screaming 'DADDY IS IN MY HAIR' after spilling his ashes into the Oregon wind. . . . We read memoirs of crisis and self-discovery to recognize ourselves and observe others. For some readers, Woolf's lacerating commitment to her truth and to refusing the good widow narrative will resonate and reassure."
　　—*The Boston Globe*

"I started reading *All of This* as soon as it arrived and quickly realized that it was going to have my full and feverish attention until I'd devoured the whole thing. It's truly a rare combination of gripping story and immaculate, genius-in-her-prime writing. I had to redo my makeup like four times during the process of reading. I just kept crying. *All of This* reminded me that honesty saves lives, and that it's an act of love to be truthful about feelings and experiences."
　　—Diablo Cody, Academy Award–winning screenwriter
　　and producer of *Juno*, *Jennifer's Body*, and *Young Adult*

"Stark, real, and very brave, Rebecca Woolf's *All of This* is one of the most true books I've ever read about grief and the relationships that bring it to us. Add to cart now because this astounding book is going to blow your mind."
　　—Claire Bidwell Smith, author of *Anxiety: The Missing Stage of Grief*

"This book is an absolute hurricane force of truth and beauty. This book takes our conceptions of love and happiness and throws them into the inferno of reality. Rebecca's writing is bloody, beautiful, and tender. *All of This* not only cracks the surface of love and relationships, it spelunks into the depths of the human heart. No one is spared, and no one ought to be. This book is a triumph."
　　—Lyz Lenz, author of *Belabored* and *God Land* and contributing
　　essayist to *Not That Bad: Dispatches from Rape Culture* by Roxane Gay

All of This

All of This

A Memoir of Death and Desire

Rebecca Woolf

HARPERONE

An Imprint of HarperCollins*Publishers*

ALL OF THIS. Copyright © 2022 by Rebecca Woolf. All rights
reserved. Printed in the United States of America. No part of
this book may be used or reproduced in any manner whatsoever
without written permission except in the case of brief quotations
embodied in critical articles and reviews. For information, address
HarperCollins Publishers, 195 Broadway, New York, NY 10007.

HarperCollins books may be purchased for educational, business,
or sales promotional use. For information, please email the
Special Markets Department at SPsales@harpercollins.com.

FIRST HARPERCOLLINS PAPERBACK PUBLISHED IN 2023

Designed by Leah Carlson-Stanisic

Library of Congress Cataloging-in-Publication
Data is available upon request.

ISBN 978-0-06-320677-9

23 24 25 26 27 LBC 5 4 3 2 1

For Rebecca

Sometimes death is the beginning of things.

ERICA JONG

Contents

Part Three

All of This

Introduction

Early on in my husband Hal's illness as we were sitting side by side in his hospital bed watching 3 a.m. infomercials to the erratic beep of the chemo drip, maniacally laughing because *what the fuck and how the hell did we get here what is happening,* Hal turned to me.

"Bec. You have to write this book," he said.

"What book?" I asked.

"The one you're going to write—about *all of this*—when I die."

It was the first time he had asked me to write about anything, let alone *him.* In the past, he was at best reluctantly supportive of me writing publicly about my life—his and ours. He struggled with my work on multiple levels, and for many years, we clashed as a result. So this felt profound. Holy. Like receiving an unexpected gift.

"Tell the truth about everything. It's okay. You have to do it. The whole story. The true story."

I promised him. But it wasn't until I actually started writing that I made the same promise to myself. I spent many months writing the wrong book—a book about *his* truth, not mine. I was protecting him, much like I did when we were married—venerating his good qualities in public forums and deceiving myself in the process.

The truth is, I am relieved to be alone. Elated to be on the other side of a relationship that broke me—a marriage that, for many years, felt purgatorial. This is not to say that my grief is inauthentic. The sadness and anger I felt, and still feel, is honest and messy and ever-worthy of sensitivity, empathy, and care. But it also looks very different than what is commonly depicted in memoirs written by grieving wives, which is why I felt compelled to write my own.

Nobody talks about what grief feels like when the person you're mourning is someone you had, for years, been preparing to lose in a different way. That a relationship after someone is dead is no less complicated than a relationship with someone who is living. It's okay to miss and mourn someone but also to feel relief that the suffering is over. In all aspects.

I am not the first and certainly not the last wife to bury a husband she didn't want to be married to anymore. Nor am I the only widow relieved to be out of a relationship that paralyzed her. But I found it nearly *impossible* to find anyone willing to talk openly about the kind of grief I was feeling when Hal died. I still do.

Widows have a long history of holding their tongues so as not to tarnish the legacies of their late spouses which, in the very nature of marriage, would also sully our own. But contrary to the court of public opinion, death does not *forgive us our sins*. And looking away from the truth will not change it. I believe we do each other a great disservice by pretending death absolves the departed—that those of us left behind must only hang on to the good. There is no right way to remember the past. It is up to every grieving person to decide for themselves what to keep of what remains.

Is it more important to bury the truth of a dead man than to honor the truth of those who survived him? I had to write this book to answer that question, and I believe with every cell in my being that that answer is no.

Marriage is labyrinthian on its best days. Even the purest of love stories are infested with idiosyncrasies; the most stable of households, flush with fabrication. In order to excavate my experience, I had to first make peace with Hal's humanity and mine. I had to give myself the space to remember him without forgetting. To love and loathe with the same level of compassion. To forgive us both by looking deeper into the story with equal parts celebration and criticism. Most ex-wives cannot write this book because their ex-husbands are still alive. It is because of them I was able to write this. Because they were brave enough to leave when I wasn't.

Months before Hal was diagnosed with terminal cancer, he got the following words tattooed on his arm: "Rather than love, than money, than fame, give me truth."

And this book is mine.

Because contrary to what women are conditioned to think, our truth is not a betrayal but an opening.

It's safe here. Come inside.

Part One

Chapter 1

Cancer Season

The stoplights are out on Wilshire and all along San Vicente approaching Cedars-Sinai. I am driving with my hazards on so the cars behind me don't honk. Hal is seated next to me, padded with pillows so the seatbelt doesn't press against his abdomen. I learned this trick after my C-section when our twin daughters were in the NICU after being born six weeks premature. It was mid-September and while I was discharged four days after their birth, they were not. For a week and a half, we spent our days driving back and forth between home and hospital—Hal in the driver's seat, me as his passenger—and every time we hit a pothole, I would wince.

"Careful," I'd say.

"Slower," I'd say.

"Look out for the—"

Bump.

That was the summer of 2011. I was in excruciating pain, but the stoplights were working. It was hot but not record breaking. And my pain was temporary. Most pain is temporary.

Now it is July of 2018 and nothing is working. The muted voices on public radio tell us *the heat this week is record breaking*. I imagine whatever supreme being who controls the weather shattering literal records one by one against the edges of dusty furniture, pieces of vinyl like broken glass under our feet. All words mean more than one thing.

Usually, when the lights go out at major intersections, there are traffic directors in green vests and sturdy hats. They stand in the middle of the road with their white gloves and tell you when to stop. But not today. Today, we are alone. Just the two of us and a pile of broken records.

I slow to a stop at every blinking light, wait for my right-of-way and accelerate through each intersection carefully so as not to discomfort Hal more than I have to. I drive fast enough so I'm not cut off by everyone who doesn't have a terminally ill husband in debilitating pain sitting shotgun in their minivan, slow enough so that he doesn't feel the bumps beneath us.

But he does. He feels every break and thump. Every lurch and snag. And everything I do is wrong. The car is either too hot or too cold. I am never driving the right speed. And now, on top of everything, the lights aren't working.

Hal's eyes are closed. He wears a mask over his mouth as a precaution against his compromised immune system even though the doctors tell him there's no need. He turns the music all the way down. It's only been ten days since his diagnosis and everything hurts now, including favorite songs.

I hold on to his hand and he smiles the way people do when they don't want you to know they don't want to. And then I do the same thing I've done every day since Hal's diagnosis: I pull my belly in as tight as I can and hold my breath. I tell him I love him, and he nods the way people do when they want you to know that they know.

"Iloveyoutoobaby," he whispers.

He opens his eyes and looks at me. For a moment, it feels like we're the only two people left in the world. And then the car behind us honks its horn.

———

It happened like this: one day he was fine, the next day he was dying.

We were barely speaking when his first symptoms appeared. Our marriage in shambles—backs turned to each other in a bed big enough to keep us from touching.

You hear stories about this kind of thing happening all the time. You know. The one about the friend of a friend who was "the epitome of health and then one day . . ."

I have done this before countless times. Someone I knew at some point in my life gets sick or dies, and suddenly I can't believe we ever lost track of each other. I think of the time we were best friends. For a summer. Or a weekend. Or during a school dance. Someone I'm pretty sure I had English with. Immediately, there's a flurry of texts with old high school friends, and "Can you believe so-and-so died so young? Remember when we all smoked cigs together when we were supposed to be running the mile and *it's just so tragic isn't it? So unbearably sad. . . ."*

And then I grieve as if we had never lost touch, marveling at the impossible distance, the time that came and went, and all that was lost in the years we didn't connect. All the could-haves and the might-haves and the maybes. *How easy it is to lose track of people*, I think. *How easy it is to lose people.* How easy it is to lose.

———

The week before Hal was diagnosed, he had pain in his stomach that he could only describe as unfamiliar. He assumed it was stress.

Because of work.

Because of money.

Because of family.

Because of me.

Days later, he went to see his doctor, who did blood work and various tests.

"Doctor called. Everything is totally normal," he said. "He thinks I may have gallstones, though. . . . Either that or I'm dying."

"You're definitely dying," I dryly replied.

Hal was always dying. When we first met, he was convinced he was terminally ill and every few months he brought it up again. We joked about dying so much it had become a sort of love language.

The doctor sent him home from his appointment very certain that nothing was wrong, told him to call if his pain got worse, if anything changed. Made him an appointment in two weeks to get an ultrasound *if* he was still uncomfortable.

Two weeks.

That was three days before he checked himself into the emergency room.

———

The day of Hal's diagnosis was a Friday. Our nine-year-old daughter, Fable, was at sleep-away camp; our thirteen-year-old son, Archer, at theater camp; and our six-year-old twins, Bo and Revie, were at skateboarding and music camps—each exploring separate passions in locations nowhere near one other. Four kids and four different camps was a multitask unto itself, but there were two of us, so we did what we always did as parents—we divided and conquered. Hal dropped our son off on his way to work and we planned to reunite later that afternoon at Revie's *School of Rock* performance at a café on Fairfax.

When we got to the venue, Hal ordered a turkey sandwich with his coffee. He hadn't eaten all day and was hungry. But as soon as he started eating, he went white.

"I think something might be seriously wrong," he said to me.

Revie climbed onto the stage, grinning at us from behind the microphone.

"Bec. My stomach feels like it's twisted in knots."

I dismissed it out of habit. Neurosis and hypochondria were nothing new. In retrospect, I think maybe part of him instinctually knew that *this* was coming. Maybe he had been preparing all along.

Revie waved from the stage and we waved back. It was the last time Hal would be in the audience for any of his children.

Later that night, he called an Uber to take him to the ER.

By habit, I turn down the radio even though there's no music playing, just silence. We pull into the Cedars-Sinai Cancer Center. Hal keeps asking for the time. He's annoyed that we are late, here, yet again, and I apologize as the valet greets us and proceeds to take photographs of my car.

I make the same joke to the valet every time.

"Ha! Why do you even bother? My car is so covered in damage you could crash it into all the things and I swear I wouldn't notice."

Hal doesn't think this joke is funny. If only the valets could see his car—nary a scratch and sparkling clean. No muddy shoes kicking the backs of his seats. No melted crayons in the cup holders or gum jammed into seatbelt holes. No bumper stickers. No rearview mirror spiderwebs caked in leaves. Hal prides himself on a clean car and the last time mine was washed was when it rained.

I pull the pillow out of Hal's lap and adjust his facemask. I sling a cooler full of pills, cold juice boxes, barf bags, and Dixie spit cups over my shoulder and wait as Hal turns his body toward the open door. He pulls himself to standing with the aid of his walker and slowly we proceed to the entrance of the hospital.

Behind us, the valet is still taking pictures.

This is only our third or maybe our fourth (or is it the fifth?) time here and we are already completely settled into the drill. Hal sits down in the lobby as I check him in. He asks me for a spit cup. (Every few minutes he gets the urge to spit, his mouth constantly filling with phlegm.)

We call for a wheelchair and wait for our transport person. I carry Hal's walker as we are wheeled down hallways and into elevators, finally arriving at our first destination—the procedure center. Here, Hal slowly lifts himself onto a hospital bed and technicians stick a catheter into his belly to drain eight liters of fluid the color of Coca-Cola from his abdomen.

On the way home, the stoplights are working again, and Hal is staring out the window of the car. We're stopped at a red on Third—an intersection we have driven through countless times before. Hal typically closes his eyes on drives to and from the hospital, but today they're open. He moves his head slowly to the side, straining, like it hurts. Everything hurts all the time but I can tell by the way he clenches his jaw that the view from his window is especially painful.

There is a couple walking down the street. They are holding hands, swinging their arms back and forth as they cross Sweetzer and hop in tandem onto the curb. They are so close to Hal's window they could touch it.

But they don't. Nothing matters outside of their moment. They are laughing with heads back and chests to the sky. And then, all at once, they are dancing. He pulls her arm, and she curls into his chest like a choreographed performance.

The light turns green and Hal cranes his neck, following them.

"Did you see that?" he whispers. "They were dancing. Literally dancing."

"I saw."

I turn the music up because I don't know what else to say. What can I possibly say? My husband is dying. He is moved to tears by two young people in love. He is crying because he's happy for them. Or maybe he's sad for himself. No, it's both. *Of course, it's both.*

———

"What would you do if you had twenty-four hours to live?" People love to ask each other this question at birthday parties or on dating apps or long drives.

"What about a week? A month? A year . . ."

I'm certain I've answered this question dozens of times, and asked it as well. It's exciting to think about how we'd spend our lives if we had nothing to lose. Where we'd go. What we'd eat. Who we'd fuck without protection.

I think about all the times I've thought casually about what I would do if given a death sentence. Like playing MASH when I was ten years old. Pick a color. R-E-D, pick a number . . . One two three . . . you will live in a shack, drive a Lamborghini Countach, marry Luke Perry, and have seventy-eight kids.

None of it is real.

Pick a cancer stage. Four. One two three four. You will die this year. You will be survived by four children. And your wife of thirteen-plus years. And the leased sedan currently parked in your driveway will be returned scratch-free . . .

. . . Because you will never drive again.

———

The light turns green and I wait for Hal to spit in his Dixie cup before taking my foot off the brake.

CHAPTER 2

Broken News

I search for my wedding ring with hysterical determination. It's been months since I've worn it—out of spite, yes, but also something else. The last thing I wanted people to see when they looked at my hands was a broken marriage—or even worse—a healthy one.

I've never owned a jewelry box. Just a dozen discarded makeup bags stained with lipstick and stale perfume samples overflowing with broken earrings. I'm the kind of girl who never grew out of cluttered drawers.

This is why I don't own expensive jewelry, wear the same necklace every day until I accidentally break it taking off my shirt. It's why most of my jewelry is knotted beyond repair and I never take my bracelets off before bed. It is also why I am on my knees at 4 a.m., flashing the light of my phone into a box of tarnished metal, shaking as I plead with St. Anthony to bring me full circle.

The summer before Hal got sick, he lost his wedding ring at an Airbnb in Ojai. The six of us had gone away after a tumultuous few months, our marriage hanging on by a thread. We were aggressive (him) and unresponsive (me), and had settled into a sort of cordial avoidance that we both recognized as complacency.

We had just moved into a new place after selling our first and only purchased house—a home I dearly loved.

But Hal was ready to sell before we even bought it. The house was too old, too broken . . .

"This house has ghosts in it," he insisted.

But I loved that there were ghosts. I loved the feeling of the old walls and how the floors slanted to the left, the cracks on the Moorish arches like tiny lightning bolts, the overgrown jasmine and the original windows, which we were told we would need to replace. (We never did.) It was a fixer-upper we couldn't afford to fix. *Like us.*

We lived there for four years before we had to sell. It was Hal's call and he was right, even though I didn't want him to be. We were broke. House poor. Falling more and more behind with every payment.

It was my fault. I had just had a very good year financially. We had not put aside what we should have for taxes and suddenly we owed the IRS fifty grand we didn't have. When we tried to refinance our mortgage, a lien had beaten us to the punch. I wanted to raise our children in that house. Prom pictures under archways. Paint stains on the driveway. All that original deco tile. Hal called a real estate agent and explained we had no choice. He was elated when he heard how much we could sell it for. I was crushed.

"As long as we don't sell the house to someone who tears it down," I pleaded. And while Hal agreed, he was also practical in all of the ways I was not. I was an idealist—believed all things would work out somehow. He seemed to always know that they would not.

A month after we sold our big, beautiful, broken house, all that was left of it was the skeleton and an arch where the front window used to be. The person we sold it to ended up knocking most of it down and selling it, brand new, for more than double what we sold it for.

Our Ojai trip was supposed to be a new start—a honeymoon for a new phase in our lives. We were once again renting and this time, thanks to inflated home prices, we had a cushion of cash. But the change in scenery was unable to change us. We fought the entire time. With the kids and with each other. We had assumed our problems were mainly financial but having significant money in savings for the first time in our marriage didn't change a thing. When Hal realized he had lost his ring, we were already packing our stuff to go home early.

I think that was the moment we both knew it was finally over. He couldn't find his ring and neither of us cared enough to look for it.

"Maybe it will turn up," I said, dragging our bags toward the car. "... or maybe it won't."

———

Now there are no bags to drag to cars. There is only this moment and this night and this life, which is suddenly in pieces. Everything is shattered—this miserable love—but fucking hell, it's still love, isn't it? Or does it only feel that way because it's suddenly clear I am going to lose him for good? My ring is missing but unlike his, I can find mine. If I search hard enough in all this wreckage, maybe it will be okay. If I can rescue our circle as the fire burns down our house, perhaps we can stand in its center again. Or, at the very least, acknowledge that what we had was beautiful once.

There is one last box of jewelry in the bathroom. I pour its contents onto a towel so as not to wake the kids with the pings of sterling silver on tile. The towel is still wet from his body, from the shower he took this morning. I can smell him in the pile of swap-meet bangles.

And then, . . . *there it is.*

———

I have a photo of all of us in Ojai the night before we left for home. You can't tell we're miserable in the photos. We look like every other married couple.

Except our hands are in our pockets so we don't have to touch.

———

I call my parents at 5 a.m. to tell them what has happened—that Hal felt sick and now he's dying all alone in the hospital. That he needs me just like *I need them, and I'm sorry to wake you, please come up.* Not one hour later, they are packed and on their way. My mother is crying on the phone in the passenger seat of my dad's car and I am trying to explain to her what is happening at the hospital. The sun is coming up and soon the kids will be up as well.

"Go back to sleep. It's so early," I say, but it's not that early. Why does the sun have to be so fucking bright?

"Mom, what's wrong. Where's Daddy."

"What's wrong?"

The words stab. The question mark like a shank to the ribs.

"What's wrong? Where's Daddy? What's wrong, what's wrong, what's wrong?"

I think I am going to throw up. Or faint. Or fall apart. But some-how I do none of these things. Somehow, I am so still. So calm. So completely in control of my feelings that I suddenly understand what it must feel like to be at war. I am steady and stable in the way people are in movies. The way people are at funerals. The way mothers have to be to break their children's hearts.

"Daddy is still in the hospital. He's really sick. The kind of sick that means he can't come home yet. And I will be with him soon. And we will be home when we can. And by then, we will know more. I love you. And Daddy loves you. And look at me, I'm right here. I'm here. Come here."

I want to tell them everything will be okay, but I know it isn't true, so I just hug them. One by one, I hug all four of them. Tell them I love them over and over like a broken record. (Like broken records.)

And I do not cry.

———

The doctors broke the news to Hal while in the hallway of the overcrowded ER. He didn't even have his own room when they told him the cancer was in his pancreas. That the cells had found their way into his lymph nodes, that his liver was covered in lesions . . .

"Pancreatic cancer in its final stage . . ."

I listen as Hal tells me what it felt like to Google his prognosis from a hospital bed parked outside the nurses' station in the same socks he'd worn to work that day.

How he had to sit for hours alone with this news in the middle of the night.

It took three hours for me to get to him. Three hours on my knees searching through broken jewelry and fixing breakfast for our children who didn't know the truth.

Three hours of my parents driving up from San Diego in the dark with bags they packed in minutes—helpless and helpful and mine.

Three hours of me trying to decide what to wear to the hospital, settling on overalls because they had the most pockets to put all of the things I might potentially need.

All of the things except my hands.

My hands would remain free.

———

I don't remember driving to the ER that morning, but I do remember trying to valet my car just as the sun was cracking its yolk over a muggy horizon. I remember the gentleman manning the station in his green polo shirt—the way it felt to put my car into park and roll down my window.

"I don't know where to park this. Can I just give you my keys?"

Emergency rooms never feel real. They are like bizarre movie sets full of people who picked an ailment out of a hat.

"And you will play the part of man howling from kidney stones."

"And you will play the role of drunk girl bleeding from the head."

I get in line behind a man clutching a barf bag to his face and try not to make eye contact. And then I leave my body. Analyze the room. The man with the barf bag represents my inability to communicate my needs and the kidney stones are the marriage I have to pass, the howling my internal monologue, all vowels.

I will play along with this hallucination for the rest of the night. I will dip in and out of whatever space exists between here and there for the next four months. For now, though, I tell the receptionist that I am here to see my husband who is "back there somewhere" and walk down the hall, past the silver-haired gentlemen with the volunteer badges. I search for the room number on the yellow sticker pressed to the front pocket of my overalls, and after going the wrong way and being redirected, I find it.

I pull back the curtain and there he is. Hal upright in a hospital bed. He has aged ten years in the seven hours since he left home with a stomachache.

I throw my arms around his shoulders and he winces, his eyes drifting down to my hand.

"You're wearing your ring," he says to me, blinking back tears.

Of course I'm wearing my ring.

Suddenly, I can feel everything. Every fight we've ever lost and every door we ever slammed and every time we walked out on each other and swore we'd never come back. All of the silent treatments and heated exchanges in the kitchen. All the love and all the hate and the guilt and the love and the remorse and the shame and the anger and the fear and the love and the love and the love. I can feel every night we slept with backs against each other and every day we didn't speak. I can feel it all pool in the space between my heart and my lungs—a well so heavy, I struggle to breathe. And then I open my mouth and exhale and it all comes flooding out of me. Guttural.

I have wanted to live without him for so long, but in this moment, I take it back.

I don't want him to die.

He can't die.

Don't die.

———

We married because I was pregnant. We had been dating for four months when, after my period was three weeks late, I bought a pregnancy test at the Rite Aid on La Brea. I didn't tell him I was taking one, but my roommate knew. He stood outside the bathroom door until my silence turned into panic and my panic turned into hysteria. I had just turned twenty-three, was hustling to make it work as a freelance writer while working nights as an online chat host for a children's hospital non-profit. I knew I wanted to be a mother someday, but not now. Not five years out of high school when I was still learning how to be an adult in the world.

But when I told him I was pregnant, I already knew the baby was mine. I knew in those first hours after taking the test, when I kept lighting cigarettes in my window and snuffing them out with my fingers. I had burns on my hands when I broke the news to him on his driveway.

Hal was seven years older than me but just as unready for parenthood. He had no money and was living in a converted pantry in a teardown house just south of Beverly. Had I not been pregnant, we would have surely broken up before the year was over. Instead, nine months after our meeting, we got married. I was five months pregnant.

I eat an egg salad sandwich while they administer him Percocet, which, for now, is strong enough to keep the pain at bay. Within hours, however, they have to put him on Dilaudid. That's how fast everything is happening. Like turning up the volume without stopping.

I want to say so many things but am afraid I will say them too soon. He's in pain and I am not. The grudges we held against each other are now meaningless. How is it possible to be angry with a man who is dying? How does one do anything but forgive? Start from scratch? Time travel back to the early days before we knew our groundwork was faulty? Would it be possible to rebuild now? *Would it be possible to create a new foundation without knocking down the house?*

"My love. Everything is . . ." But I can't finish the sentence. I cannot tell him it will get better. I am unable to lie, so I lie down.

"I'll never take it off again," I say, clutching my ring.

"I'm going to die from this," he says back.

———

That night, I make out with Hal in his hospital bed—the first time we've done that in many years. *The greatest love stories have the worst timing.* But there's another part of me that thinks I cannot trust myself. What if this is just me performing like I believe I'm supposed to. I am a character in a movie now. Tragic. Hysterical. Seemingly scripted.

"I'm not going anywhere, do you understand? I will stay with you until the end."

It is the only marital vow I didn't break.

———

I pretended I could wait it out. *When the last kids go to college . . .* I'd say to myself. *I just have to get through these next twelve years.*

We struggled financially from the beginning. My success was sudden and unexpected and caused rifts early in our relationship. I felt as pressured to provide financially as I felt punished for being the primary breadwinner during the years he was in and out of work. In the early days of my blog monetization, I was one of the lucky ones, pulling in six-figures a year writing about a life I originally wrote about for free. In the early 2000s blogging was my hobby—I never anticipated that by 2007, it would become my career. I was also the primary caretaker of our children and the only one of us who could *handle* being up all night with our babies, especially the twins, for whom I spent more than a year sleeplessly caretaking while he slept soundly in our bed.

Hal didn't have the patience for night feedings or night changes or any kind of all-nighter at all, so I took on 100 percent of the responsibility. His sleep mattered more than mine. He had to get up and work a *real* job. It took me years to recognize how often I accepted such patriarchal defaults as truth—the resentment in me silent, but building.

Our marriage was stable only when I was willing to do everything in my power not to trigger him. We were sustainable only when I was willing to smile and wave, to pretend that everything was fine, to lie to his face.

If I wasn't making enough money, he was angry. If I was making too much money, he was angry. Devil's advocate was the only role he knew how to play with me. So in the last year before he died, when I stopped blogging and started focusing on my own side-hustle projects—occasionally writing copy for a handful of clients and creators—he became furious that I was suddenly so flippant about our finances. He interviewed for a second job he didn't need because I wasn't making enough, and at night, when I was putting the kids to bed on my own, he sat up in the dining room and worked, headphones on, blocking me—and all of us—out.

He didn't have a choice, he told me. Who was I to argue with him? I didn't even have access to our finances to tell him what we could and couldn't afford.

Money, they say, is the number one cause for divorce but, for us, it was more about the inequity, the imbalance—what happens when one person is able to follow her dreams and the other is not. Hal was a musician who came to Los Angeles to perform, to entertain. To be a star.

Instead, he got a girl he barely knew pregnant. Had to get a day job with benefits.

And although he climbed the ladder from production assistant to producer, it was never the work that he wanted to do. And every night, over dinner, I would hear about it: the job he took for the family. He would come home angry and take it out on me—on all of us—repeatedly—until, eventually, it became mundane.

In the beginning, when we were both struggling equally, we were okay. And I guess I just assumed if we could make it with nothing, we would always be able to make it. Just like our parents. And our friends. And all the many married people in our lives.

If they could *stay together for the kids*, so could we.

I was conditioned to believe that, as a mother who placed her children's worth above all else, I was doing them a favor. By martyring myself, I was giving my kids the ultimate gift—my happiness in exchange for theirs.

Our marriage was a tourniquet I didn't think we could live without. I had convinced myself that loss of circulation in my limbs was a small price to pay—that my options were to bleed out or lose the feeling in my legs.

I had become proficient in the poetry of acceptance. I accepted that my marriage was hard. That unhappiness was what they meant when they said, "marriage is about compromise."

And perhaps it was—even is—for some people.

The truth is, I wouldn't have survived the next twelve years. Hal wouldn't have either.

When we finally sat down to talk about separating, he was already feeling unwell. He was dying and neither of us knew. Our marriage was over, and we were trying to figure out how to successfully split as he played down the dull pain in his lower abdomen.

We stopped saying "I love you" to each other. Even in passing. Even before bed, when in the past we would mumble "I love you" against our pillows, flapping our hands toward each other in a sort of "I'm too tired to touch you right now" salute. I prayed for something to happen—a windfall, a lottery ticket—a message that said

YOU CAN GO NOW. YOU HAVE TO GO. So when Hal called from the hospital to tell me that something was terribly wrong, I imagined myself at the bottom of the sea, pulling various messages from bottles so that all the ones I had sent out as SOSs would be lost, destroyed, proven to never have existed.

Still, my friends and family knew we were irreconcilably broken and that I had been chipping away at my marital escape for years. It would be presumptuous of me not to believe that he had been, too.

It took me over a year, with the help of a lawyer, to gain entry to our savings accounts after he died. He refused to give me or anyone access to so many things, including the bitcoin he'd invested in which I was never able to get to at all.

"I don't want to deal with this right now," he told me every time I asked. "We'll talk about this later."

But we never did.

I justified his unwillingness to help me prepare for a life without him as a symptom of the cancer, but of course I'll never know. Maybe, in the end, he was tired of doing everything for his family.

And by the time he was near death, he had had enough.

———

The morning of Hal's forty-fourth birthday, he wakes up to blue skies and a seemingly unlimited view. The doctors gave us the okay to go home for a few days to celebrate his birthday with our children, who are still unaware of what has transpired over the last thirty-six hours. We want them to hear the truth from us, face-to-face.

Not a single thing I brought to the hospital has been touched. I pack a dozen more hospital bags in the next four months and it is always the same. Magazines. Books. Changes of underwear. Soft T-shirts. None of it will ever be unpacked.

Hal asks me to take the lotion from the hospital bathroom, *and don't forget the socks.* The socks are bright yellow, the color of caution tape, with sticky grips on both sides that resemble tread. These socks will become the only constant through his illness. He will die in these socks and then someone will throw them away.

He doesn't look sick. Not yet. He is able to walk out of the hospital without assistance. He puts on the sneakers he wore to the ER and checks his phone as I collect paperwork for the discharge. He is going home with only a handful of prescriptions. For pain. For constipation. There are scrips for symptoms that have yet to reveal themselves. I take the notes the nurses give me in the hallway. I am introduced to a team of social workers. Everyone keeps asking if I'm okay.

I have spent years breaking down over relative nothingness, but in the hallway I become someone else.

We are going home to tell our children that their father is dying and then we will celebrate his birthday. We will eat cake and take a family outing—wherever Hal wants to go. We will toast to what it means to get older knowing now that he won't. And we will mourn the birthdays he will never see.

Music will swell. Credits will roll. I tell the discharge nurse that I'm fine.

———

How do you prepare to tell your children that you're dying? You don't. Which is why we say nothing to each other in the car, look ahead as we drive straight home. One intersection at a time.

I pull the car into the driveway. Turn off the engine. He looks at me and I look back. These are the last few minutes of their childhood, I keep thinking. Inside, we will draw a line that will differentiate one of their lifetimes from another. We will break their hearts.

"Let's make a plan for after," he says. "Maybe we go on a family walk."

"Whatever you want to do," I say.

"It's your birthday."

Later that day, we will take our last walk as a family to the Los Angeles County Museum of Art. We will press the admission stickers to our chests and dance around the sculptures. Hal will walk the entire time unassisted, stopping only to marvel at all the healthy people who are not dying. He will ask me *why him,* and I will say *I don't know.*

And then he will laugh, like *can you believe this is happening? What a world.* And I won't know whether to laugh with him, so I will smile and say "I can't believe it either, baby."

And he will tell me he likes it when I call him "baby."

And after that, I won't stop.

But before that . . . before the museum . . . and the birthday cake . . . and the candles going out in the darkness, he sits us all down around the dining room table.

He announces that he has something he needs to tell everyone. And then he breaks the news himself.

"I am sick . . ."

". . . I am so sick that I am dying . . ."

". . . I am so sick that I am dying and I'm going to die . . ."

He speaks tearfully in one run-on sentence. No commas. No periods. Only truth.

He proceeds to go into detail about everything that has transpired over the last few days. First, the ER visit, then the various scans, the doctors telling him he has cancer. He tells the kids he doesn't know how long he will be alive.

"But we are a team," he says, as the ceiling caves in.

"And we always will be." His words are like rocks against the windows.

"Even when I can't be here . . ."

And with that, our children have fallen into the floor.

"But look at me! Right now, I am here. Do you see me? I'm here. I'm alive. Look."

I open my arms as our children climb out from under the pile of rubble, gasping for breath.

Half of our kids are in my lap and the other two are with him. We all hold hands.

And I forget all the things about Hal I despised. Every layer of accumulated dust is up and gone—vanished like the lives we led before now.

That's when we fold our bodies sideways and re-open like flowers. We are being born again together around a dining room table we bought on sale at a store that was going out of business. Archer was a baby then and the table matched his highchair.

One by one, the children ask if he will be alive for their future milestones. Archer's graduation from high school. Fable's fifth-grade run for student body president. Bo and Revie's tenth birthday. He smiles at every question, tears rolling down his cheeks, and shrugs. "We don't know what's going to happen to any of us, ever. Even when we're healthy. Even when we think our lives will look a certain way."

And everyone, all of us brand new, understands.

———

I never loved a man more than I did the moment Hal broke the news of his death to our children. I would have died for him in that instant—sacrificed every part of myself to see him live and love and thrive.

It was as if the man I always knew was in there somewhere was released into the wild—exposed and unafraid. His prognosis had fractured an exterior that could only give way in this circumstance. That's what it felt like. Like, *here he is—opening.*

This is the man I was waiting for—the person I could have sworn was here all along. I just couldn't get to him. All that digging and clawing and begging for all those years and no dice.

Is it possible? That in dying, we find our purpose? Our life force? Was this what was happening? A man coming to terms with his softness after years of being hard?

He was glowing. The most beautiful man I had ever seen. Father of my children, love of my life. The crack in his exterior had found its way to mine.

It is possible to hate a person with your entire body and also love him with the whole of your heart.

There is a picture I have of Hal blowing out the candles on his birthday cake. His eyes are closed, and the room is dark except for the flames. I took the photo moments before his breath extinguished the fire. I often think about what it must have felt like for him to close his eyes and make a birthday wish knowing it was likely his last. What kind of wish does one make when their time is suddenly running out? I never asked. How does one ask? There were so many things I didn't ask.

Later that night, I try to hold him, but he is in too much pain to lie down. Instead, he sits upright against the green of our headboard and we hold hands. Stay up all night. Watch *L.A. Story* as the sun is coming up—his idea. He wants to watch something we have never seen together before.

We say nothing to each other, our eyes glued to our shared distraction. I had forgotten about this movie with its freeway signs. Their godlike communication, cryptic advice. And I watch them intently, hoping they will tell me something important, too.

"So what do I do?" Steve Martin asks the sign after it tells him he's in trouble.

"U will know what 2 do when u unscramble 'how daddy is doing'," the signpost replies.

Hours later, we are back in the ER. But before that, we share a joint with the door closed, like we did when we first met in the summer of 2004. Before the fights began and the all-nighters. The dreaded nine-to-fives. Before we grew to disagree on almost everything. When we were both freeway and sign.

We don't know what's going to happen to any of us ever. Even when we're healthy. Even when we think our lives will look a certain way.

CHAPTER 3

Hurrycanes

I have heard from people who regularly experience hurricanes that there's an eerie calm before they hit. A calm that feels like adrenaline. Like, *okay, but is it really going to be that bad? Looks like clear skies ahead.* Some people even race to the beaches, defiant of Mother Nature's warning: *don't make me count to three.*

I've heard that, sometimes, even after it's reported that 100-mile-per-hour winds are on their way, locals will offer death glares to blue skies, nudge trees like, *well, if this thing's still standing after a hundred years of storms . . . if she didn't bend, neither will we. We'll ride it out, that's what. You don't scare me, Mama.*

I've never been in a hurricane, but I think I understand. I've been warned of a thousand DANGERS AHEAD, shrugged each one of them off. *Worst case scenario, I'll have a good story,* I'll say to myself. *Worst case scenario, I'll be picked up by the wind and taken somewhere I might never have seen otherwise . . . follow the yellow brick road.*

I'll leave my sunroof open as a dare. Tell the clouds to come at me, bro. Beyond ignoring warnings, it's very hard to imagine that weather can change so much so fast.

Outside of the sudden pain in Hal's abdomen, there were no cancerous symptoms up until the diagnosis. Even his blood tests came back normal. Nothing to see here. Clear-ass-skies, that's what's up.

And then, not forty-eight hours later, it started to rain. The day we came home from the hospital, he started pissing blood. The day after that, his belly swelled up like a woman in her third trimester. *The wind shook the windows.* He started to hallucinate. *The door blew open.* His skin turned yellow. His pain became unbearable no matter how much weed he smoked or how many Percocet he swallowed.

Suddenly, it was time to evacuate, but he couldn't leave his body. Not yet. Instead, he lived within the confines of a category 5 storm for nearly four months. We all did. That's what terminal cancer is like. A hurricane from which you cannot evacuate.

A land that you dream of once in a lullaby.

Somewhere over the rainbow . . .

Red the color of urine. Orange the color of eyeballs. Yellow the color of skin. Green the color of vomit. Blue the color of bruising. Purple the color of feet so swollen they crack like eggs.

———

They discharged Hal from the hospital, thinking he was ready to come home. But one day later, I take him back. I had spent the night before leading him in Lamaze breathing. I didn't know what the fuck else to do. The kids were pretending to be asleep and Hal was howling in pain like an animal hit by a car.

"You gotta help me, Bec," he kept pleading, but there was nothing I could do to help him. *There was nothing I could do to help him.*

Not even Google or the reflexology chart I pulled up on my laptop and tried to follow—so many pressure points—gave me any answers.

"Okay, but maybe if I . . . let me try one more thing."

But it was too late. The storm was here. It did not take a turn once it hit land. Instead, it picked our house up off its foundation and threw it into the sea.

———

They move us from the ER quickly this time. The receptionist asks what we're here for and I tell her my husband has pancreatic cancer and he needs to be admitted right away. Hal shifts his weight in the wheelchair I asked for upon our arrival.

They don't even make us wait.

His room is on the fourth floor, which I soon learn is the floor where they treat cancer patients and only cancer patients—no kids allowed. *You must be eighteen to enter.*

I read the sign and try not to think about what this will mean later on.

The smell is familiar now, even though we've only been here once before. Hospitals become familiar very quickly, probably because everyone is always smiling at you and saying things like "good morning" and "that's a pretty blouse" and "which floor?" Soon I feel comfortable within these walls and forget there is even a world beyond them. I step outside and immediately feel lost, wandering the parking lot looking for my car. I fumble with the lock before climbing inside, throw it into neutral instead of reverse. *Vroom.* Whoops. *Just kidding. Nothing to see here.* I won't even think to turn on music or the AC. Instead I sweat through my clothes in the bloated silence of my minivan.

Cedars-Sinai hospital is located on San Vicente and Beverly, the intersection of my adult lives. I spent my early years in LA at the Beverly Center. I drove to Urth Café from my apartment in West Hollywood. Wrote at Insomnia Café on Poinsettia. Brunched at Lulu's when I finally made friends. I don't think I went anywhere that wasn't on Beverly Boulevard my first five years in LA. Maybe

Melrose. Or Fairfax. Or The Burgundy Room on Cahuenga back when you used to be able to smoke inside.

Now, though, at thirty-seven years old, there isn't a road I spend more time on than San Vicente between Olympic and Sunset. I have been driving it at least twice a day since 2010, when Archer started kindergarten. We are lucky the hospital is so close to school. So convenient. Not many people can see the roof of their children's school from their husband's hospital window. Not many children can see their father's hospital room from the upper yard where the tetherball courts line the fence.

Its "convenient location" will become something else after all of this is over. It will become the place where Daddy died. For now, though, my kids wave when we drive by the hospital.

"Hi, Daddy," they say, rolling down the windows.

"We hope you feel better, Daddy!"

There are other, longer routes we could use to go home, of course. But taking a different route would suggest we are unable to acknowledge the truth. Taking a longer route would mean looking the other direction. No. This hospital is part of who we are.

I became a mother in that hospital, and I will become a widow there, too.

———

Hal gets into his new bed on this new floor with the new IV and the new smells and the new dry-erase board with newly scribbled names. They administer his pain meds immediately and his entire body relaxes.

"I hope they let me stay longer this time," he says. "I don't want to go home."

I look out the window and wonder if there's a new mother downstairs looking at the same sculpture garden I can see. I wonder if she's holding her baby like I was a little over thirteen years ago, twenty-three years old and petrified. I say a prayer for her, this invisible woman who I have decided absolutely exists. I pray that hospitals only ever remind her of giving birth, that she has someone nice to drive her home so she can sit with the baby in the backseat, hold its tiny, wrinkled fingers, unafraid.

I turn away from the window and toward Hal.

"You don't have to do anything you don't want to do, okay? You don't have to go home."

———

Captain's Log: Night seven on this cot with these beeps and these sheets and this bed alarm that I keep forgetting is on. I went thirty-seven years before I knew what a sponge pop was. I dream of tap dancers and wake up to rattlesnakes in the morphine drip.

"Fall Risk" it says on the door and the floor and the hospital bracelets.

Two mornings ago, I woke up to the howls of the patient next door.

"Help me," he said. "I feel like I'm going to die."

"Sir. You have to be more specific."

———

I have a list going in my phone and it says things like "contact Trevor at Equinox and tell him what's happening. Tell him you need to cancel my membership." I copied this down verbatim based on Hal's wishes.

In the early days of his diagnosis, he has all sorts of demands and I'm relieved. I want him to tell me what to do. I want him to bark orders at me like a boss in a bad movie. I want him to tell me all the people I have to call.

"Tell my spin wife I have cancer. Give her my info." He was referring to a woman he was close friends with at his gym. A woman I did not know and had never heard of. I cannot remember if I ever called her or what I said to her if I did. I know I didn't write her name down. Sometimes I think about her and whether or not she even knows where Hal suddenly went. There were many people like this, who didn't know that Hal was dead until months, even years later.

It is very hard to cancel a gym membership. They are the Hotel California of subscription services. Once you're locked in, you're locked in for life, and sometimes longer.

When I call Equinox to explain to them that I have to cancel my husband's membership, I am told I need a doctor's note.

"I need a doctor's note that says he's dying? I am with him in the hospital. He cannot walk, let alone take 6 a.m. yoga classes. He can't even fucking stand. You think I would make this up?"

The man on the other end of the phone doesn't know what to say to me. He puts me on hold and then hangs up. Maybe an accident, but probably not. I call back.

"Hi. Me again."

"Oh, yes. I am so sorry. I think we were disconnected. Please hold."

This will be the first of many cancellations. I will spend hours— maybe even hundreds of them—*explaining*. First with doctor's notes, then with death certificates, saying thank you when people trip over their condolences. Answering questions over and over because people cannot help but want to know how young people die. They need to know what they can do differently as not to meet the same fate.

I will go from carrying a red notebook to a blue folder to a canvas bag full of everything I need to close accounts and then open them. To prove that a man existed and then didn't. That a wife existed and then didn't. That a family existed one way and now looks like something else.

"Do you mind if I ask how he died?" "Do you mind if I ask how old he was?" "Did he have any symptoms?" "Did you see it coming?" "Do you mind do you mind do you mind . . ."

And I will become more callous with each call and each meeting and each day. I will walk into offices so stoically that strangers will bristle at my shields. Like, look at this bitch. She means business.

Because there is no other way to handle a death.

We stole the walker from the hospital. Hal's biopsy results were still pending and there was a chance—albeit small—that his tumor was the good type. The Steve Jobs one. The it's-still-possible-to-live-several-years-Whipple-procedure kind. So we held on to that. We told the nurse the walker belonged to us and winked at each other when she left the room.

"Oh, this walker? Is TOTALLY ours," I said. "We've had it forever . . . I mean . . . it feels like forever. You know what I mean. Ha ha. Anyway . . . this ol' thing? Nyuck, nyuck." A future full of adventures was limited, clearly, but that didn't mean we couldn't still be the Bonnie and Clyde of medical supply theft. Desperation is why people steal.

Not that we were actually stealing. We were borrowing. When someone is dying, everything is borrowed. It's not like I was going to keep the walker as a souvenir.

In the end, I would leave it behind. With his body and the bed-ding I brought from home because the hospital sheets weren't soft enough.

———

We found out Hal's cancer was the bad one. The you-probably-will-die-before-the-year-is-over one. There would be no Whipple procedure. No surgical removal of any tumors, liver or otherwise. There was only the option of chemo treatments, which probably killed him faster, if you want to know the truth. But he wanted to do them anyway. The doctors said it might help, so he said yes and he said yes and he said yes.

"Whatever will give me more time."

Desperation is why people steal.

———

The day after we came home from the hospital the second time, a physical therapist came to the house. She was one of many who did house calls when Hal was not hospitalized, and when she saw his walker with Dixie cups taped to its feet, she frowned.

"I need two tennis balls and a sharp knife," she demanded.

Hal nodded. He had just bought two new packs, he said.

"They're in the garage, I think."

He was right. They were the first things I saw when I entered the garage. Freshly purchased, along with a pair of rackets for the girls. I ripped the top off a three-pack and brought them back inside along with a sharp knife from the kitchen.

Hal grew up playing tennis. His summers were spent hitting balls at the local tennis club. He competed throughout high school, earning a tennis scholarship that he later declined so he could focus on music. When we first met, he talked about tennis all the time—his first love.

We played tennis together once. But he was so good at it, and I was terrible. The balls were going everywhere, and I couldn't control how hard I hit them. After that, we never played again. Sometimes it isn't a match and there's nothing you can do but say "good game" and put the rackets away. Sometimes it's better not to even try.

Why we were so good at calling certain matches but not others is beyond me.

I could think of nothing that made Hal feel more alive than tennis, which is why something broke in me when I passed the balls and knife to the physical therapist. I knew what she was about to do. And I knew what it would mean to him to watch her.

After Hal's initial acceptance of his diagnosis came a rejection of unsolicited emotions. He explained that he was feeling enough pain as it was and couldn't bear to see anyone else distraught. This included his parents, his children, and me.

In those first few weeks, it was understandably common for visitors to break down upon seeing him. *How could a man look so unlike himself so fast?* It was also unfair for him to have to pacify those who clearly needed calming, which became a job I was more than happy to take on. It gave me purpose, even, to be the one to hold everyone's hands.

"I can't handle anyone crying in front of me," he had told me. "Please make sure everyone knows to leave the room if they're going to cry."

And I did. Mostly. Even when it didn't feel right. He was a dying man, and I wanted to respect his wishes as best I could.

Which is why as soon as I handed over the tennis balls, I left the room.

Slumped against the door, I covered my ears as the physical therapist stabbed each tennis ball with the knife I use to cut bagels. That's where she found me twenty minutes later.

"You okay?" she asked.

"Yes. Is he?"

"I want you to order him a cane so that he can work on his walking when he's feeling up to it."

"But what about the tennis balls?"

"They're fine."

It was called a *Hurrycane*, which we thought was cute at first, but later on, felt like he was being mocked. No one walks quickly with a Hurrycane. Are you cane manufacturers fucking kidding me?

Hal was really good at slowing down. He didn't get frustrated the way I thought he would when he was doing laps down the hallway and back with his cane or the walker with the murdered tennis balls. He placed each foot carefully in front of the other, his eyes fixed on the point ahead, round the dining room past the kids who looked up from their markers when he asked them what they were working on.

"Shhhhhhhhh," he said, when they started answering all at once. "I need quiet . . ." and then he was gone before they could answer. *It's okay, he doesn't really mean it. You can keep talking. It's not you. He's just in pain . . .*

The longer he was away at the hospital, the harder it was for him to come home. He did not have the tolerance for voices, even when they belonged to his children. He reminded the kids that he was sick and needed to be alone. Or worse, he asked for me to bring them to him and then immediately changed his mind.

Perhaps it was too painful, or maybe it was something else, but one day he woke up a patient and that was all he could be.

He knew exactly where to put his shrinking body, how to lift his knees over the pillows, and take one step at a time. He knew how to hold up his arms during a sponge bath. How to look away when

I injected blood thinner into his shoulder with a needle the doctor taught me how to use. He knew how to pretend not to care about the tennis balls.

He became a savant when it came to hospital equipment, decisively rejecting the first two hospital beds that I ordered, but not until they were fully installed in our bedroom.

"I want the same bed I have in the hospital or else I'm not coming home," he told me, which I soon learned was almost impossible. It is very hard to find an actual hospital-grade bed to rent. They can be purchased, of course, for around ten thousand dollars, but renting them is a very different story.

After spending an entire day calling every medical supply store in the LA area, I finally found a bed that was *almost* the same bed he had at the hospital. "But you better come soon because someone else already called about it."

I called my friend Alexa, who lived so miraculously close to the store it felt like a sign, and not ten minutes later, there she was—all ride-or-die, model poses against the blue plastic of the mattress. It was a Hill-Rom, the Cadillac of hospital beds: a cool $1,300 a month to rent. Because, of course, insurance wouldn't cover any of it.

It was delivered the next day along with a side table identical to the one Hal had in his hospital room. From there, I bought the same green-apple juice boxes he was served, the same Dixie cups he was given his meds in, the same '80s medical chair he insisted on having at his bedside.

———

There's a tree on our street—towering—maybe an oak or something like it. It was one of the tallest trees in the neighborhood until the morning when, out for a walk with the dog, I find it severed in my neighbor's front yard. There is blackness in the wood where it split. Like someone set its middle on fire.

I am struck dumb looking at this tree—her remaining branches, strong and full against the sky. Crows, oblivious, claw at her viridescent leaves, crowded and panting, breathlessly alive.

There is no sign of foul play. No storms have come through here. Still, she is a dying thing. It didn't matter that her roots were tough enough to split sidewalks or deep enough to pull water from the neighbors' soil. Something made her sick from the inside.

And by this time next year, everything, including her birds, will be gone.

One of the oddest things about death and dying and people getting sick is that everything else stays the same. The kids still have summer camp on weekdays and need to be dropped off and picked up. They all get hungry. Sisters fight over the remote. The trash still needs to go out on Wednesdays. The dog can't wait for her walk at 5 p.m. *Welcome to today*, I think upon rising every morning. Now, take a breath and push open the door. Turn on the lights. Fill the cup with ice. Err on the side of levity. Find peace in surprise. Observe how healthy-looking trees get sick, too. Even when they don't look like they should or would or even could, they can.

Branches snap. Bellies catch fire. Nests come loose. Still, we must go on walks before dinner.

My dad returned Hal's car to the dealership for me. I couldn't bear to do it. In Los Angeles, our cars become these extensions of self. Our mileages, memoirs. Every dent and scratch and registration sticker. All the meetings we take on speaker phone while commuting. Hours of our days are spent driving in cars we assume won't outlive us. Hal wouldn't even outlive the three-year lease of the car he was so excited to drive off the lot. The car he kept spotless, except for the scratch on the left front bumper which was (of course) my fault. The car with its glove compartment like a five-star restaurant bathroom—Tic-Tacs arranged with gum, all color coordinated.

I was able to empty it out, but barely. Collected the CDs from the trunk. His gym bag. His collection of quarters. I put everything in a brown paper bag and then stuck it in the trunk of my minivan. Almost three years later, it's still there. The bag. I think I'm afraid to touch it. There are so many things of Hal's I'm still afraid to touch.

The day my dad returned his car, I sat in the grass outside of our house and watched him back it out of the driveway. Hal was dying and all the things he loved about being alive were disappearing one by one.

Now I was the only one left who could drive.

That was the end of the Hurrycane, as well. Its tenure was short, but it didn't seem like it. The days were so long, so full of every possible feeling and terror, that the weeks with the cane felt like much more. Hal went back to using the stolen walker with the slit tennis balls. A double homicide keeping him upright. A theft allowing him to move forward.

I kept the cane, though. And the medical chair Hal insisted we buy. The chair my friend Jasmine found at an AMVETS for a hundred dollars marked down from $875.

We returned the hospital bed the day before Hal died. It was my mom's idea. She had his bed and side table and all of his medications and medical equipment removed so that when I came home to our bedroom it would be mine.

The chair and the cane are still in the garage. Sometimes the twins sit on the chair for fun and rock back and forth. Sometimes they play make believe with the Hurrycane—pretending they're old ladies, hunched over with one hand on their backs.

"Deary," they say to each other. "Wait for me, Deary."

"I'm coming, Deary. I'm coming."

———

I sleep in the hospital with him.

It's more selfish than it sounds. I cannot sleep unless I'm here. I try once to sleep at home and can't do it. Feels like I can hear his moans from miles down the road.

I co-slept with my babies for the same reason. I strapped Bo to my chest in an Ergo and lay flat on my bed, fell asleep only once her body relaxed—her fisted hands softening into tiny fronds. Even now, I cannot fall asleep until I know my children are tucked safe and sound in their beds.

Some nights, I sleep next to Hal but mostly I sleep on my cot, shoved between two walls so the nurses can get around me to take his vitals every few hours. Sometimes they whisper, ask if I need anything and I say *no, thank you.* Sometimes they say nothing, and I ask how he is.

"His vitals, I mean."

While he's doing chemo, I'm not supposed to use the same bathroom, so I use the one in the hallway—brushing my teeth there every morning and then again at night with the other partners of patients and power of attorneys. Once, I slipped and called myself Hal's POW instead of his POA and the woman on the other side of the counter didn't even flinch. She knew what I meant and that it was the same difference anyway.

Sometimes I can feel the POW's in the hallway. They are forming a neat and orderly line behind the locked doors, toiletry bags in hands, toothbrushes with square plastic hats, and the kind of disposable wipes people bring on camping trips.

Occasionally, someone will knock even though the door is locked, and I'll have to say *hold on one second. I'm still in here, be right out.* Those who attend to patients are often the most impatient. Caretakers have nowhere to put their anger, that's why.

I come to appreciate the hospital late at night. It feels like I'm sneaking out into a world I don't belong to every time I leave Hal's room. I clutch my toiletries to my chest and eavesdrop on all the nurses' stations. Some of them know me by name and come out to say hi as I make a joke about the toilet paper attached to my flip flop that I didn't notice was there until now.

"Thank you, thank you! I'll be here all night!"

I continue down the hallway, past elevators and beeping machines and nurses whispering in the common area, its lights like Las Vegas, with winners and losers and bathrooms that smell like shit in the morning and toothpaste at night.

Except this casino is nothing but clocks.

Hal opens an eye when I enter his room and then closes it. Nods.

"Goodnight," he says to me, his hands folded over his chest. "I love you."

We are so good to each other like this, I think. We are the perfect married couple. And all it took was a hospital gown and two different bathrooms.

"I love you, too," I say, climbing into my cot, its coils clicking beneath the weight of me like a slot machine.

Chapter 4

In Sickness and in Health

For the first days after Hal's diagnosis, I was convinced it was my fault. That all those years of wishing he would *leave me* led to this. That all my inadequacies as a wife, as a partner, had made him sick. That the rage I'd caused in him had hardened into tumors.

I was the cancer. I was the metastasis. I was the Wicked Witch of the West.

Except the house fell on him instead of me.

I started cheating on Hal within two years of being married. I never thought I would stay but I didn't know how to leave. We had a baby. I didn't want to split custody of our child. So I left in other ways, convinced myself that the only way to live truthfully was to be myself in private.

One cannot be judged by her truths unless she shares them aloud, and a liar is so much safer, so much easier to love. So I buried my secrets like treasure in the backyard. Way out by the fences I pretended I didn't know how to climb. The problem was, I forgot to eat the map.

I don't know if it was the first time he went through my email. I do know that, nine years into our marriage, he finally found what he was looking for.

I wasn't home when Hal opened my computer and went digging in my drawers, but I imagine what he must have looked like—his fingers on my keys, face pressed against the windows of words intended for someone else.

When he rang my phone to call me out, I was on set standing on an apple box, moments away from delivering a baby food–sponsored monologue, smiling into a camera like the whore he would say I was later. Reading off the teleprompter, pretending to be a good wife to an audience of strangers.

"I know everything. I read everything," he screamed. "And I'm leaving. When you come home, I'll be gone . . ."

I scrambled to turn the volume down on my phone, assuming that everyone could hear him. And then, before I could respond, he hung up.

"Rebecca? Is everything okay?"

"Yes. Everything is fine," I said, before delivering the monologue to the camera—my smile, a smear of saccharin.

I'm just a lying liar who tells lies.

And the show must go on.

We decided to marry in Vegas because that's where liars who don't want to get married get married. It's where newly pregnant, barely adult women stand in line with other newly pregnant, barely adult women. It's where gamblers say "I do." In Vegas, a wedding is a song lyric, a punchline, a double dare.

Not a single person was invited to our wedding. The big-haired receptionist guest starred as our marital witness. She smelled like baby powder and cigars. "Y'all from around here?" she asked upon signing us in. I don't remember where Hal said we were from, but I know it wasn't true. He was a liar, too.

A Vegas wedding with no witnesses is like a tree falling in a forest—no one there to hear it make a sound. Without witnesses, it felt like our wedding was pretend. That we were just a couple of people who ran away for a weekend and then came back with matching tattoos.

If a father isn't there to give his daughter away, does that mean she gets to keep herself?

I was five months pregnant when we exchanged vows on the stained carpet of the Little White Chapel. I wore gray pants and an off-white maternity shirt covered in flowers with a pair of sleeves that opened wide as mouths. My something-borrowed was the baby in my belly. My something-new was the lump in my throat.

"In sickness and in health . . . 'til death do you part. I do."

They pronounced us Mr. and Mrs. before he kissed the bride. But I was never going to be either of those things. Not a Mrs. and certainly not a *bride*.

I hated every minute of our wedding. I found out later that Hal did, too, but for different reasons. He wanted a real wedding with real flowers and real people we knew as witnesses.

When I married Hal, I chose to keep my father's name over his, but only because it was my mother's name, too. Woolf had become me. She was the only Rebecca I knew.

We made a compromise. The child I carried would have *his* name so that *I* could keep mine.

Going along with things I disagreed with was an integral part of my marriage, but only because it was how I'd learned to be loveable in my formative relationships. Boys always liked me because I did all the things they wanted girls to do.

Because agreeable girls become lovable women. All you have to do is say yes.

But over the years, the shift became seismic. My internalized bitterness became a passive aggressive time bomb, and by the time our twin daughters were born, I was furious with myself for not fighting harder for our daughters to take my name. Wasn't that fair? For our son to take his father's name and our daughters to take mine?

It mattered to me more than almost anything. How could I raise my four children to be patriarchal rule breakers when their very names were yet another example of *a wife placating her husband*? Another woman who cosigned for the erasure of her lineage because of some antiquated rule?

"Then just change their names already! If it means this much to you, just go change their names."

But I didn't and I wouldn't, and he knew that, too. I would never change my children's last names for the same reason I would never change mine.

And yet the moment I knew he was dying, the moment he called me from the ER the day before his forty-fourth birthday with the stage four cancer diagnosis and "Bec, this is it. I'm going to die . . ." The moment I hung up the phone, I had one thought: I'm so glad our children have his name.

———

"This is the wrong juice, Bec," Hal snaps, recoiling at the taste. He's drinking out of a Dixie cup with a blue monster on the side.

We have been back and forth between home and hospital so many times I've stopped counting. I have a garbage bag full of discharge paperwork under the bed as proof.

In order to come home—to stay home—Hal insists he needs everything that is available to him at the hospital to be in our house, including the juice boxes the nurses mix with his constipation cocktail. Ocean Spray green-apple juice in tiny wasteful boxes mixed with MiraLAX. Cold. But not on ice.

It's the same with the straws that bend at the tops and the chicken salad he orders from the hospital cafeteria.

When we are home, everything I do is wrong. Even when I do *everything* exactly like the nurses told me, taught me, walked me through with pen and paper multiple times. I understand why. I will survive this and he will not. I am fine with being a punching bag. Welcome it, even. It makes me feel less guilt for having a healthy, working body. For knowing that I am the one who, goddess willing, will see our children off into adulthood. I am the one who can stay and I am sorry. So sorry.

"You're doing it wrong!" he screams at me as I pull the plastic sleeve over the chemo port in his arm in preparation for his shower.

"Just stop! Don't even bother! I want to hire someone else to do this."

The day the homecare worker comes to bathe Hal, he fires her before she can grab the soap. Seated naked on the shower chair, clutching the plastic sleeve over his port, he tells her to "get my wife and go home."

———

As a teenager, I was the *cool* girl. Not because I was *cool*, but because I let the boys do whatever they wanted and thanked them for it. They could talk shit about girls in front of me and do things to my body and ask me for favors and I always said yes and *like, totally, for sure.* I cooked and cleaned and drove them around in a car I filled with my own gas money. I was the pit in which to bury secrets, desires. I was free therapy. A sex worker who didn't need to be paid. Worse, there were many times—too many to count—when I paid them. "Oh, you're low on money? No problem. This one's on me."

I protected them. Stuck up for them. Got them job interviews. Helped with their homework. Told them to call me if they needed anything. Always picked up.

This is nothing new, of course. We know exactly how to give it all away and then apologize when we give it away *wrong*. We amputate our arms when asked for a hand and are *so very sorry* for all the blood.

We are women and this is what we have been programmed to do for generations. Like taking last names without compromise. And being *given away* by our fathers at weddings. A platter passed between men.

"Can you please pass the meat?"

"Sure. Let me wrap her in lace first, because purity. Because virginal. Let me cover her face and mouth with white, because lamb."

And yet, I have always cried at weddings even though every single one of them makes me want to stand up and scream NOOOOOOOOOOOO.

At twenty-three, I didn't know how to scream yet. I never wanted to be anyone's wife, but one day I was going to be a mother and Hal was going to be a father and even though we barely knew each other, we got married. Because that's what pregnant women are supposed to do. Because I loved him. And he loved me. And maybe that was enough. *I assumed it was enough.*

We loved each other madly, in those days—the way people do when they first meet. When the sex is insane, and everyone is still pretending. I knew how to be the woman he wanted me to be. I was passive and kind, thoughtful and generous. I cooked beautiful meals every night and fucked all morning. And he made me laugh. He was funny and charming, charismatic and sexy. He was confident and interesting and wild.

I was already pregnant by the time we had our first fight but didn't know it yet.

"I don't believe in art," he had told me. "I believe in entertainment."

"But I'm not an entertainer, I'm an artist."

"Do you sell your work?"

"Yes."

"Then you are an entertainer."

Every time I opened my mouth, his voice got louder. It was the first time I remember feeling afraid of him. No one had ever talked to me like that and I froze. Did the thing that I would do a thousand more times over the next decade: swear to leave. But I didn't. Instead, I said nothing as he went deeper into his monologue about art and commerce and why I was wrong. And when he was done, he immediately changed the subject. Like nothing had happened. Like *everything was fine, moving on*.

This fight would come back to haunt us repeatedly through our marriage. I was almost always wrong about everything, mainly how I perceived my work, my art, and myself.

He had opinions so strong his voice quaked. And every fight ended the same way: with him relieved to have gotten whatever he was ranting about off his chest. And me beaten the fuck down, alone in whatever corner of the room he'd left me.

He knew everything and I knew nothing, and because he was so much smarter than I was, I believed him.

―――――

The day Hal broke into my email, he found what he had always assumed to be true but had never confirmed—that there were lovers, local and distant, who I had fucked behind his back.

He was looking for one man's name in particular. Someone who had, years ago, sent a letter to my post office box. It was a beautiful letter, tender and sexy—like the emails we'd been sending back and forth for several years. We rarely saw each other in person and the intimacy of handwritten words became a lifeline. I could have just as easily thrown away all evidence of our tryst, but I didn't want to. He was a secret, but he was *my* secret, and having tangible proof that he was real felt like a necessity. So, I stuck the letter in my wallet, in the slot where I kept my credit cards, and that's where it lived for more than two years.

I had forgotten it was there until the day it flew out with my credit cards, my daughter's doughy, toddler fingers opening the note like a present in slow motion.

I watched without reacting, afraid that my expression would become notable evidence of wrongdoing. I could feel Hal's eyes on me as I pretended not to notice.

"What do you have in your hand?" he asked our daughter.

And that was how an innocent messenger handed over my secret life.

I watched him read it, squinting, his hand over his mouth, the nodding head.

"Jesus Christ, Bec."

"The letter is old, and we no longer speak," I lied. "Please believe me."

He just looked at me. Stared.

I denied everything, of course. Swore on bibles I didn't believe in. Pleaded with runaway words, excuses, and stories. Excused myself for some air only to come back and continue. . . . He knew I was lying but I refused to tell my truth. If I broke my secret world open, it wouldn't be mine anymore. It would be dead. I would have to find a new yard to bury my skeletons.

Several months later, Hal broke into my emails. Not in a moment of passion but as a premeditated plan. He knew I was going to be out all day working so he decided to call in sick and break down my doors. He later justified his invasion by telling me he couldn't take it anymore. He had to know the truth.

And the truth is what he got. My emails were just as vulnerable as the letter in my wallet. All he had to do was search for recipient names that started with J. I imagine it only took him a matter of minutes to find our years-long exchange. Dozens of emails about all the ways his wife had fucked around with someone else.

I was a cheater. And in another time or a different place, I would have been killed for what I'd done. Burned at the stake. Stoned to death. Strangled by my father. Perhaps this is why I didn't feel the guilt I was programmed to feel.

I had been unhappily married long enough to recognize the affairs of women for what they almost always were: an escape.

Show me where the adulteresses go to hang their heads in shame and I will build a pedestal for each and every one of them.

That night, as I waited for Hal to come home, the big tree in our backyard uprooted for no reason. The symbolism fell like a shadow over our broken home. But the tree meant something different to each of us. He didn't want a reason to leave, so I sat him down and arranged the entirety of my bones at the foot of the bed. Pulled skeletons from once secure locations. Gave all my secrets away.

Every man. Every affair. Every time. Over and over and over.

I should have felt relieved. Instead, it made me feel something worse than guilt. There was a wildness to me that I felt fiercely protective of and now it was his. He had hunted for it, shot it dead, held it up for me to see. He had broken into my secret life—the only place I felt safe from him—and burned it to the ground.

And I wasn't sorry for any of it.

That didn't change the fact that Hal had every right to hate me. *Of course, he did.* I was a cheating wife. Not just once, but many times, with multiple people over the course of our marriage. I had affairs when we were happy and when we weren't speaking. During good times and bad. In sickness and in health. I couldn't keep it in my pants, and I was never going to be the kind of woman who wanted to. I was at my best in casual relationships. It was so much easier to be honest with people who didn't love me and never would.

I wanted an open marriage from the beginning, but the few times I tried to approach him with nonmonogamous options, it turned into the kind of fight I knew better than to revisit. If my truth was a trigger, why tell it at all?

I think many women are like me. We have been brainwashed to feel so ashamed of our truths that we lie in order to live. About who we love and how. About the kind of love we want in return. We have been lying as a way to preserve ourselves since the beginning of time. So when we tell each other to be honest—woman to woman— what we are really saying is . . . it's okay. You can tell me your secrets. You can share with me how you stay sane.

You can tell me how you lie.

———

The night of Hal's diagnosis, I was handed an advanced care pamphlet and the first of what would soon become a stack of similar-looking business cards, the words Cedars-Sinai in elevated red text. Inside the pamphlet were forms I was asked to sign, notarize, and return "as soon as possible" regarding "organ donation" and "do not resuscitate" and "what to do with your loved one's remains."

At first, I didn't know if Hal *wanted* me to be his power of attorney. How does one trust an almost-ex?

But he trusted me. He knew, in the end, I would take good care of him.

I would stay as long as he was sick. I told him this repeatedly—made sure he never doubted it was true. Because it was true. *It was true.* **It was true.** But it was also true that I knew he wouldn't live much longer. That navigating his death with grace meant I could keep one vow. That in the end, I would get what I wanted all along: to be without him.

CHAPTER 5

Future Exes

I do not believe that there was anything particularly abnormal about our marriage. I have known enough wives in my life to know that this is the case. We crushed each other's hearts and spirits in ways that were, at times, comical in their banality. I broke promises. He broke me. We were always deeply flawed, which may explain how and why we fell in love after first having hated each other the moment we met.

Across a café in early 2004, our unlikely pairing was masterminded by a mutual friend who knew Hal wanted to write a TV pilot about suburban teenagers, but also knew he would need to partner with a writer—someone like me. And while I should have known better than to join forces with someone who, while full of brilliant ideas, was seeking someone else to execute them, doing the bulk of the work for half the credit was par for the course at the time.

I was there first, uncharacteristically on time, and Hal was late. I knew it was him based on the way he had been described to me and when he walked through the door in bell-bottom jeans and a tight, black T-shirt covered in teddy bears, I audibly gasped. Was he joking or was this some sort of statement? It was impossible to tell with him, which was part of his unconventional charm. His fashion was the height of early aughts—masculine "metrosexuality" hijacked by a sort of Goodwill-meets-warehouse-rave, topped with a page boy cap and a blue bandana he wore underneath.

He was cocky and loud and disinterested in hugging me hello. Instead, he threw his hand out as a sort of social-distancing maneuver. He was exactly the kind of guy I despised and, judging by his reaction to me, I was similarly disappointing. We had the kind of meeting people joke about later.

"Oh, yeah. We fucking *hated* each other when we first met. Total mismatch. We were vibrating in two opposite frequencies from day one. Cancer/Gemini shit."

I found him as abrasive and overwhelming as he found me stuck-up and condescending. But he was also charming in a way I didn't want to admit. Charismatic, his body tanned and lean like a dancer. I would find out later that his "leanness" was actually caused by starvation. He had been living off ramen noodles and malt liquor from the 99-cent store, which is where we spent our first date.

This, of course, became part of the appeal for me. He was another one in a long line of broken boys I could nurse back to health.

We were always opposites, making zero sense to one another, but that was, perhaps, why we were able to love each other the way we did. It can be easier to love the things you know you'll never understand. Or maybe the hate we felt for each other in the beginning was the part of us that caught fire. Perhaps that's why we couldn't stop it. Why I spent many many years afraid to try. Either way, by the time we went to New York together two months after meeting to celebrate Hal's thirtieth birthday, I knew I loved him. And I knew that I had never felt that way about anyone else before.

Two months after Hal and I met, I told my brother over AOL chat that I was certain Hal would father my children. And when Hal was dying, my brother found and sent me our exact exchange. It was like a message in a bottle from a past life that I needed to remember in order to take good care.

This was one of many souvenirs friends and family went digging for when Hal got sick. There were emails and videos, old photos, and letters full of memories for me to read to Hal "if and when he was up to it"—stories I had never heard before, had no idea about, letters I read quietly while Hal was *resting his eyes*. This is the beauty of dying. You get to attend your own funeral in a way. Friends come out from all stages and phases of your life to remind you who you were and are and always will be to them. Artifacts are pulled from their museums and mailed in large envelopes with extra stamps.

Hal wasn't interested in looking, but he was open to listening to the videos friends sent from their apartments and houses, in their cars, and on their walks to work.

"I love you, man," they said. He smiled. Nodded. Closed his eyes.

Even the less pleasant memories became love filled. Like disasters that sometimes evolve into your favorite stories to tell at dinner parties. Like falling in love, years later, with a bad tattoo.

Do you remember the time we were in Maine with the kids and everyone was lost but we kept walking down the path and through the woods to where we could see the ocean? I have a picture of you leading the way. That's the kind of person you are—the kind that people follow. You have always made it easy to believe you. To trust that you know the way to the lighthouse. . . .

Or the day we went to a sculpture garden and the insects were buzzing and the flowers were prickly against our ankles and we kept finding ways to be alone? I think of the garden often, even when things were really hard and I didn't think we should be together anymore. I think of what it felt like to be alone with you in the middle of all those copper sculptures and wildflowers and how nothing mattered outside of the way we made each other feel. On that trip, I was blissfully happy in a way I might never be again. We called each other "my one" and fantasized about the hundred lifetimes we'd live together. The places we'd travel. The adventures in store. . . .

A month later, I was pregnant. Two months later, I peed on four sticks and they all showed double lines. Six months after that, we were married. Ten months later, we were parents. Do you remember? Everything happened so fast.

———

Weeks after we started seeing each other, Hal introduced me to his old friends over a dinner neither of us could afford to pay for by calling me "his future ex-wife." It stung at first, until I realized he was only saying that because he loved me and was scared of what that meant. I loved him, too, but my feelings never scared me.

Perhaps that was our greatest difference.

He called me his future ex-wife on and off for the entirety of our marriage. He claimed it was *just a joke* but, over time, it became comforting to hear him say it.

"Don't worry. One day you won't have to deal with me anymore."

"You promise?" I would dryly respond, but we both knew I wasn't joking.

We replaced what good we had in our marriage with jokes about what a mess it was. We *hate each other . . . ha ha . . . marriage is the worst* became our mantra. Sarcasm was our love language. It worked for a while—the jokes and the insults and the eye rolls. The refusal to do anything for each other unless it was for a laugh at somebody's expense.

Sarcasm became our emotional drawbridge. I could tell him that he was the worst and he could tell me I was impossible, and we didn't have to take anything seriously unless we wanted to.

I hate you, when said with a smile, can mean many things.

While Hal was dying, my brain was like a funeral slide show of our best-ofs. Every conversation I had with friends, with family, with his nurses, and doctors centered around Hal's wonderful qualities—his brilliant mind and offbeat humor. His charisma and charm, his magnetism. I wanted him to be remembered for all the qualities that made him loveable. I wanted to absolve him of his misgivings and salute him for his many strengths. I wanted to praise him like a good wife. I wanted people to know he was a good father. That he tried his best. That he was a good father who tried his best. I wanted people to know that I knew he loved me. That his children knew he loved them. I wanted to paint the portrait of the kind of father and husband dead men are supposed to be. So, I revisited our life together, gathering up his greatest hits.

I emailed myself photos of him that I loved. Videos of him playing music with our children. One in particular became a touchstone. He is playing guitar outside in front of a blazing fire. The girls are half naked dancing around him, twirling against the light, their shadows tall against the flames. He's playing "Patience," his twang a perfect Axl Rose.

Said woman take it slow and it'll work itself out fine
All we need is just a little patience . . .

I tried my best to breathe and *stay in the moment*, to be all the things I knew he loved about me when we first met. Steady and calm and hospitable, like the mother I was before we had children. Like the *wife* I was before we married.

For much of our relationship, I was enamored of the full circle of it all. The way the beginnings and endings seemed to touch. Hal gave me shit about it—my constant state of childlike awe at life's many call backs—all the proverbial wheels that turned through every intersection, milestone, marker. Signs, I called them. But they were always more than signs, they were patterns. Rhyme schemes. Poems that wrote me back.

"You and your full circles, Bec," he said.

In that way, it wasn't a surprise that our marriage—which happened because of a surprise pregnancy—would end with a surprise death.

"The real shocker in all of this is that I'll never get the chance to be your future ex-wife."

I made sure he knew that while I wasn't always capable of taking care of him the way he wanted me to—the way I did when we first met—I was here, now. I knew how to do this part. I wasn't scared.

"Just like you promised you'd do in the beginning, when I came to your house in the dead of night, hands overflowing with pregnancy tests. When you looked me in the eye and told me it would be okay. You weren't afraid, do you remember? We would make the best of a life neither of us was prepared for . . ."

You and your full circles, Bec.

CHAPTER 6

Punchlines

Hal wears the same hat every time he goes in for his paracentesis. It says I LOVE YOU across the front. Fable bought it for him for his birthday so he can carry her love with him when they aren't together. He wears it because he wants people to know he loves them, too. When the valet helps him out of the car, *I love you.* When the receptionist is checking him in at the procedure room, *I love you.* When we are in the elevator with strangers, *I love you.* When we are parked in front of the cancer center waiting for the valet to bring the car around, *I love you.*

I try not to take it personally that the love he has for everyone else—for strangers and acquaintances we meet in elevators—seems to eclipse his love for the people he's closest to.

I know from experience that sometimes it's easier to be vulnerable with strangers than with those you care about the most.

———

On appointment days, when it was time to get his port dressing changed or his belly emptied or his chemo pack filled, Hal either gazed up at a random stranger, smiled, and said *I love you*, or he scowled, sneered, and spit into his cup. He was like a dog who knew immediately upon meeting people whether he wanted to bite them or wag his tail. Like his filters had been stripped completely. He was primal now.

But the men who parked our car for us were special. They were young and vibrant—their muscles chiseled and heaving under tightly fitted polo shirts, biceps glistening in the summer sun. They were as alive as men could possibly be outside a cancer center—the patron saints of health. A line of golden gods.

Sam was built like a linebacker. His brown eyes were deep and kind and he spoke with a gentle, thumping voice. He was the valet Hal bonded with the first day we pulled into the cancer center and on appointment days, the person Hal was most excited to see. Sometimes, before we had even parked, Hal rolled down the window and called out to him like a little boy.

During our first appointment, they talked a bit—about football, mainly—which, in the end, was the easiest topic of conversation for Hal to hold. Football kept his mind clear. It was a world detached from the life that was leaving him. And as a New York Jets fan, he related in a whole new way to their history of bad luck and losing streaks. Pancreatic was sort of the Jets of cancers. The best you could do was win a few games but, more than likely, you weren't going to make it to the playoffs.

Sam would crack a joke about the game, hold out his hand, and lift Hal's shrunken body into the passenger seat—the tenderness of two men with bodies that once resembled each other.

After our last outpatient appointment before Hal was admitted into the hospital for the last time, Sam was there, too. He saw us in the lobby as I was filling out paperwork at the front desk and asked if he could take Hal to the car.

I hung back by the desk after the paperwork was signed, watching as Hal and Sam's mouths moved on the other side of the window. They appeared to be talking about something of great significance, the kind of conversation that should not be overheard.

By the time I was outside, Sam had removed Hal from his wheelchair and was clutching his entire body in his arms—jaundiced skin clinging to bones like spilled yolk. I had never seen a man hold another man in that way. Like a father holding the limp body of his sleeping child.

I waited for Sam to place Hal in the passenger seat of my car before climbing in myself. Hal had tears running down his cheeks.

"I love you, man," he whispered, hand against his heart.

"I love you, too, Hal," Sam said back, clutching his own chest in solidarity.

Perhaps they both knew the Jets would lose again. That there was no way to change the trajectory of bad luck.

———

I get a call as I'm checking Hal in. One new appointment has been added to our schedule. "I don't understand," I say to the receptionist on the phone, "why do we need to meet with a genetic counselor?" But as soon as I hear myself say the words, I already know.

I tell Hal we can't go home quite yet.

"I'm staying right here," he tells me, hunched over his Dixie cup. "I'm not going to the meeting."

"Are you fucking serious?"

It is the first time since his diagnosis that I have allowed myself to get angry like this to his face.

"Go talk to her outside," Hal says.

In my head, I slap him clear across the face. I pull him out of his wheelchair and drag him by his arms out the door. I have never hated him more than I do in this moment. Which is why I don't leave the room to cry.

The counselor agrees to meet with me in the hallway, which is where I take my seat—alone, like Hal was when he first found out he was dying. I know the news is bad, so I lean into my tears. It is the first time I have cried in the cancer center and I feel that after two dozen appointments in more than three months, I have paid my dues.

"I'm so sorry," she says, handing me a tissue.

She goes on to tell me what I instinctively know. That Hal's tumor tested positive for a genetic abnormality common for Ashkenazi Jews. BRCA2, known as the *breast cancer gene*, was made famous by the bravery of Angelina Jolie's prophylactic mastectomy, an experience she went public with in 2013. At the time, it was controversial. A powerful woman and sex symbol removing her breasts so not to contract the same cancer that killed her mother. *But she's so beautiful*, people said. *How could she?*

She wrote, "On a personal note, I do not feel any less of a woman. I feel empowered that I made a strong choice that in no way diminishes my femininity."

I remember reading her powerful op-ed and thinking to myself, yes, as a mother, of course I would do the same. I had never for a moment thought that there was a possibility my daughters would grow up and have to make such a decision.

"There is a one in two chance your children will be carriers as well. How many children do you have?"

"Four."

It is hard to see one's babies as adults, let alone grown women having to make choices to remove parts of their bodies in order to live.

"Can I hug you?" she asks, and I tell her *of course yes please and don't let go* and then I apologize for getting mascara on her cardigan and she tells me not to be sorry and I say, *thank you, yes, that's what I always say, but right now I can't help but feel so sorry for everything and everyone and, oh god, My kids are going to lose their father and now this. NOW THIS.*

At least I am crying in a hallway full of strangers who understand. They don't even look at me, that's how much they understand. When you are familiar with pain and grief and genetic counselors there's no need to stare. I get it. I'm just like everyone else here, trying to stay positive while clutching folders full of bad news.

"Here's my card. Please call if you need anything.," the counselor says, my face still buried in her neck.

I compose myself before returning to Hal. He is alone in the room waiting. I wipe my hands on my jeans and tighten their grip around the handles of his wheelchair.

"What took you so long?"

It's a good thing he is dying otherwise, I might have killed him right then. In the middle of the cancer center, my arms full of genetic tests.

"You want to know what took me so fucking long?"

He is covering his ears, telling me over and over to stop. He doesn't want to know, and I refuse to acknowledge his hands as shields. He is in a wheelchair—vulnerable, frail, dying—and I am torturing him with this news. But he has to know because he won't be here when I am faced with the repercussions of the same gene that will kill him. He has to parent with me. Right now. Against his will. For the last fucking time. And I'm not sorry. Do you hear me? I'm so mad and I'm so sad and I'm not sorry.

"Your tumor tested positive for BRCA2, the breast cancer gene. Which means our children will have a one in two chance of having it as well. Which means . . . which means . . . which means . . ."

His eyes don't leave the wall. He spits in his Dixie cup. He waits for me to stop crying and then asks if we can go home now.

"That's it?"

"I want to go home. NOW."

"They cannot be tested to see if they carry the gene until they're eighteen. I will be their only parent then. Please be with me now. Please, just this one last time . . ."

But he can't. And he won't. And there is nothing I can do but let it go and drive him home.

This is the moment I became a single mom.

———

I apologized for Hal a lot in the beginning of our marriage. Made excuses for the times he raged at me or the kids in front of other people. My job was to diffuse—to sense when a valve was loose and to back away slowly, talk in a soft voice so as not to trigger his rage. To make jokes. To take the kids for a walk. For a drive. To close the door.

"Sorry. He's just tired."

"He's stressed, you know. Work has been tough."

"He's not usually like this."

I was mortified when he acted like this in front of people, not because I was embarrassed by him, but because I was embarrassed that I "chose" this. I chose a life with a man who yelled at his children in public. Who yelled at me in public. Who *yelled*.

"Shhhh, everyone can hear you," I said, more concerned with other people than anything. He never laid a finger on me—on any of us—but his anger became our invisible monster. *Don't you dare wake it up.*

He scared me for years, until one day he didn't. There was no inciting incident. One night I just fought back.

I had run out of quiet excuses so I threw my head back and screamed.

Hyperventilated until I puked. Told him not to touch me when he tried to calm me down.

"Don't you fucking DARE."

At the time, I thought I was being brave by sticking it out. By staying together for the kids. But it isn't brave to sit passively in your misery.

It isn't brave to model the acceptance of toxic relationships to one's children. To fake it till you make it work.

I had confused sacrifice with cowardice, empathy with denial.

It is never the "right thing" to stay with the wrong man.

The bravest women I know are not widows. They are divorced.

I wheel his chair down the hall of the cancer center. It has only been one month and I have already memorized the complex maze that is Cedars-Sinai—the way the procedure center connects to the rest of the hospital and how we have to walk various halls underground. There are windows in the ceiling, a reminder that even down here there is a sky.

I am sniffling. He spits. Asks for the water, which I bring with me everywhere. Water and juice and snacks in case he wants to eat. Straws so he can drink. Dixie cups. I carry medicine and an ice pack to keep everything cold. I carry barf bags and facemasks and his copy of *Still the Mind* by Alan Watts. I am a new mother again, and must remember to bring everything with me when we leave the house.

We drive home in silence. Music off. I come home to my children and wonder if, somewhere in those perfectly alive bodies, there are cells plotting their attack, learning to be cancerous, inching their way out of hiding, watching the clock. I look at my children's father's body deteriorating in real time—bones emerging so quickly, I swear you can see them move through his flesh.

I wait for Hal to fall asleep and then go to them one by one and tell them what I now know to be true.

That when they turn eighteen they will have the option of being tested for a gene called BRCA2

That being a BRCA2 carrier will mean special treatment and possible surgery. That we will figure it out together and do you have any questions I love you so much.

They all respond similarly. With questions and bravery. Just like they always have.

I show the girls photos of prophylactic mastectomies and explain to Archer what a BRCA diagnosis means for males. (Men who are BRCA2 carriers have a higher risk of prostate, breast, and pancreatic cancers, as well, but the female reproductive system is so vulnerable to this specific gene mutation, some women have upwards of a 70 percent chance of getting breast cancer.)

I tell them that no matter what happens, I am with them, we are a team. That we will know how strong we are by remembering how strong we've always been. That there is no permanence in any of this. Or any of us.

"This is all part of the adventure," I say, holding their hands. "At least now we know, right!? All we can do is move forward. Everything is temporary. I'm here with you."

Look at me. I'm here.

I do not bring the BRCA test results up again. Come morning, I rub Hal's swollen feet like nothing happened. And he thanks me like nothing happened and we smile at each other like nothing happened.

And I forgive him silently as I administer his daily blood thinner. Squeeze what fat remains on his arm and inject him like nothing happened.

Numbness, I have learned, is contagious.

People come to visit. Family. Friends. Some from far away. They fly west to California to say goodbye to their nephew. Former roommate. Best friend.

I escort every visitor into his room with a warning.

"Sometimes he gets angry."

I apologize for him.

"He's just uncomfortable."

"He doesn't mean it. Not really. He's just . . . passionate."

"He's just . . . tired."

"He's just . . . in pain."

"We know," his friends say.

They are here for closure, to say goodbye to a man who was once more alive than any of us. They are here to say goodbye to the person they loved who looks like someone else now, to say, "I love you, man," and to hear it back.

But Hal isn't ready.

I don't blame him. *Remember how we used to leave parties when no one was looking?*

"Let's sneak out the back and no one will notice," we said.

I hate goodbyes, too.

I want him to feel loved and comforted and comfortable—to listen to music that calms him and to eat the foods he craves. I want every day to be less painful than the day before. I want to give him the greatest end of life that I possibly can. Of course, I do. But nothing feels good to him. Nothing tastes the way he thinks it will. His cravings last only until the food is put in front of him and then he makes faces and pushes it away.

Like the time he asked for grape soda. Welch's if possible. In an ice-cold glass bottle.

"It's all I can think about," he said.

So, I sent an SOS to family and friends and suddenly a hundred grape sodas arrived, and he was like, *what the fuck, Bec. I don't want this.*

"But you said . . ."

"Well I changed my mind."

We want what we can't have until we can have it and then we don't want it anymore. I know. I get it. We're all the same. But this was something different. An unappeasable desperation. All of his earthly needs were insatiable. He texted me links of impossible-to-find snacks from his childhood. Or he'd order random things off the internet. One day, it was a PlayStation. Another day, it was an Alfred Hitchcock box set. And then there was the bonsai kit for beginners.

Was it comforting to order things online and have them appear like surprises? And what was it about the trees?

"I want to learn something new," he said, his eyes widening as I sliced open the cardboard box with my car key.

"Maybe it's something you could do with the kids . . ."

He shook his head. It was just for him. He wanted me to close the door behind me so he could be alone.

He never planted the trees or even learned how to grow them. He never watched a single Alfred Hitchcock movie, nor did he open the box set, which, to this day, still rests with dusty edges in its plastic tomb. I have almost gotten rid of it on several occasions, but it feels like sacrilege, at this point. Same with the unopened grape soda and *Bonsai for Beginners*.

What if one day the kids ask about the trees and want to grow them on their father's behalf? What if they ask for artifacts of their father's dying and death and I have to tell them I threw them all away? What if, instead of the closure they never received through their father's passing, they find it in his copy of *Rear Window* or *The Birds*?

That would have been me, I think. Collaging together all the clues. Who was my dad if not for the tangible items he left behind? Why else would he have purchased so many seemingly random items only to leave them unopened? Unwrapped? Perhaps these were his last words to his children.

Learn to grow your own trees.

Drink the grape soda before it expires.

———

We used to joke that we did everything backwards. First comes the baby in the baby carriage. Then comes marriage. Then comes love. This felt like a continuation of everything happening in reverse. First, we decide to get a divorce. Then, never mind, one of us is dying now. It would read like a comedy if it wasn't so tragic.

Which is why, in the end, that's what we did. We laughed at the vulgarity of dying as the nurses sucked bile from his belly.

"I said no foam, barista!" we shouted as they drained the coffee-colored liquid from a hole next to his belly button. Foam bubbling against the lid. Vat after vat.

One night, I walked into his hospital room and found him blasting *Figaro* from the speaker of his phone, his eyes closed, like he was a character in a movie. I wrote it down because I wanted to remember it. There are some things about dying that are so beautiful, it's hard to even explain how they make you feel.

His final days were like pages in a book that have since been glued together. I have attempted to perform surgery on said pages by going back into the archives of my notebooks and photographs, screen grabs and text messages but I know that even still, my translation is off. It is impossible to write about things exactly as they were. I cannot think of a more unreliable narrator than a miserable wife who becomes a redeemable caretaker who becomes a grieving widow within the span of four months.

I recognize this as I go through every note I wrote while Hal was dying. The Instagram posts I asked his permission to publish. I question everything now. Who I was writing for and why.

Death is so final, it's no wonder we strip it of its nuance. Tell the story we know that everyone wants to hear.

It is so easy to sympathize with a widow who grieves the way she is supposed to grieve. It is even easier to write the stories we are expected to tell.

Everyone is so afraid to say the wrong thing, so they say nothing. Not of death or disease or the messiness of terminal illness and what a body looks like when it deteriorates like a time-lapse video: tragedy plus time.

One of the last songs I played for Hal in a room full of people in the days before he died, was *Die My Darling* by the Misfits. No one in the room thought it was funny. But I did.

And so did he.

Die, die, die, my darling

Don't utter a single word

The more unrecognizable he became, the more I imagined the way he looked when we first met—American Spirit cigarette pressed between the final fret on his green painted Yamaha guitar. Laughing and strumming and playing along.

They say that hearing is the last sense to go before we die. I knew he couldn't smell or taste or speak or feel with his hands. But I knew he could hear me . . .

I'll be seeing you again

I'll be seeing you in Hell

My laugh underneath the verse of the song—an inside joke that made the whole room uncomfortable.

Hal loved the Misfits. He used to play their greatest hits on his guitar. And he laughed and sang with an elongated twang. The ash from his cigarette hitting the strings as he banged chords, his voice emulating Danzig's to a tee.

I was asking him to die.

Don't try to be a baby

Your future's in an oblong box, yeah

That's what you're supposed to do, you know. You're supposed to stand around the man you built a life with and tell him it's okay to leave it behind. To let it go. To die, die, die, my darling. Loud against the quiet. Silence versus noise. Tragedy plus time equals white light and loud music and death as the punchline of a joke that is only funny to those who understand.

Don't try to be a baby

Dead-end girl for a dead-end guy

And some will not.

Family in the room looked at me like I was crazy. Like I was losing my mind. And maybe that's because in so many ways I was. So much of me was merged with him. So much of my brain and my body and my adult experience. Our home, family, children, fourteen entire years of my life. Everything that mattered to me, was his, too.

Don't try to be a baby
Now your life drains on the floor.

Tough crowd, I remember thinking, my phone held above my head, singing along to the lyrics.

"You guys don't know this song?"

But this was exactly Hal's humor, and, oh god, it was mine, too, and all at once I realize how lonely it will be without him. A decade and a half of inside jokes gone. The disappearance of references to shit no one but us thought was funny.

This was it. The end of our bizarre love language. He would die and I would go through the rest of my life alone with our sardonic quips now one-way tickets to destinations unheard of. No one alive to understand.

And so, as Glenn Danzig blasted above us in a room overflowing with family members perfumed in Purell, I said a prayer.

That somehow, in some distant '80s-era punk rock heaven, we would find a way to meet in the afterlife and sing the living shit out of the Misfits' greatest hits.

Die, die, die, my darling . . .

In harmony.

. . . I'll be seeing you again.

With Hal on guitar.

Chapter 7

Sleep Talking

They started almost immediately after his diagnosis. Verbal, mostly, and always when he appeared to be sleeping. Haikus from the outskirts of consciousness.

Sometimes he woke for a few moments, looked around the room, then resumed what I assumed to be rest only to boldly come alive with pantomime. At first, I thought he was joking. Messing with me.

"Hal? You talking to me?"

But he never was. Not really.

My Uncle acted out in his sleep in the same way before he died. He appeared to pick up fishing poles and fly fish, holding the invisible rod with one hand, winding the reel with the other, and then in one dramatic motion, casting the pole toward the same yellow hospital socks.

Hal played piano against his chest. Sometimes guitar. Other times, his hands rose from the sides of his body slowly, like he was trying to lift something fragile. There was also pointing. To the ceiling, mainly. Sometimes out the window. He nodded his head and moved his hands like he was trying to say something.

Often, he woke himself up. Opened his eyes.

Did I say something? He would ask.

"Yes! You were just talking about racehorses. Or music. Or food that you wanted from the school cafeteria. Or how idiotic white people are who call the cops on Black people for no reason."

Sometimes he apologized for the things he accidentally said, but there was nothing that came out of his mouth when he was seemingly unconscious that was offensive or mean spirited. Just these tiny nuggets of magic and sorrow, joy and truth.

". . . give me truth."

Hal was always a talker. He talked so much that I had stopped listening to him years ago. Now I was desperate to hear from him, hanging on his every word for answers, closure, anything. So after about a week or two of "You okay? Hal? Are you talking to me? Do you need something? Should I call for the nurse?" I shut my mouth.

He started to do the thing with his hands where he looked like he was building something, and I watched and listened and took notes.

He reminisced aloud in his sleep. Most of his early stories had to do with being a teenager in the summer. About cold sodas on the fourth of July and how even the air tasted like barbeque. The boys were unselfconscious about the way they smelled playing carnival games. Trying to win prizes for the pretty girl named Jessica. Sweat coming through their shirts as they shot water guns in the direction of the bull's-eye only to come away with a stuffed animal small enough to fit in the palm of a hand. *Ding ding, everyone's a winner. Even you, teenage girls.*

Then there were the live goldfish. Easier to win and often dead by the end of the night.

"We carried them in our backpacks in plastic bags tied at the tops. They only leaked a little," he explained.

Hal had a thick head of hair at fifteen and wore it long down his back and over his eyes so that he had to hold it back with one hand when he was going down hills on his skateboard. Or maybe it was his bike?

I sniffed at the him in the descriptions. The way he used to smell before the hospital. Before the peppermint lotion and antibacterial wipes. Before the Purell and urine. His natural odor combined with Old Spice was some exotic recipe for something resembling home. I never got tired of whatever pheromone he gave off. Even when I hated his guts, I sneaked up behind him when he came home from the gym, placed my face in the crook of his armpit and inhaled. On laundry days, I gathered up his T-shirts with both arms, plunged my entire face into their filth, and moaned.

After he died, I continued to sniff the armpits of his shirts. The ones I never washed. The ones I still have hanging in the hallway closet between our eldest children's rooms. Because here's the thing: his body is still in those shirts. It's why I haven't gotten rid of them even now, years later. His body is everywhere in this house, the fragments of a ghost who's still invited to dinner.

Smells go away though. Where to, I don't know, but one day I went to huff Hal's shirts and the heaven in them was gone. And I fell to the floor like that scene in *American Beauty* where Annette Bening pulls her dead husband's empty button-downs from their hangers. Like, *wait. Don't go. Not like this.*

I found out more about Hal's childhood while he was sleeping those final weeks than I did over the course of the past fourteen years. Nostalgia made him uncomfortable when he was healthy. When we moved in together, the only pictures he had of his life before our meeting fit into a single manila envelope. In contrast, I had about twenty boxes full of journals and every note I ever exchanged in middle school. Perhaps this explains the shirts still hanging in our shared closet and that I still have every one of his shoes, even the ugly ones. I have worn them all, just in case he can feel the LA sidewalks under my feet.

I realized quickly that the words Hal said while unconscious-ish might be more valuable than the ones he said while lucid. He wasn't angry in his sleep. Or in pain. He was thoughtful and insightful. He was a poet. I started to wonder if maybe *this was real* and everything else was pretend.

Perhaps death is where we get sucked back into our truth like a dream we wake up from and then fall back asleep to find. Like a Saturday morning with no alarm. Over the years Hal had become more and more detached. At the time, I assumed it was because of me and us, but now I wonder if it was more than that. He had been very sick for a long time. Many years, the doctors said, and perhaps there was a part of him that knew that. Like the way dogs start to ignore you in the final stages of their lives. One of mine did that. She became withdrawn. Stopped sniffing on walks. Went the other way when the kids wanted to pet her. Hid behind the house to be alone.

When I told the doctors about the conversations Hal was having in his sleep, they corrected me.

"Delusions. Those are called 'delusions.' You shouldn't let him talk like that. You need to reorient him. Next time he starts talking about the past, remind him where he is."

"Why would I reorient him to *this*?" I asked.

"So he knows where he is."

"Why would he want to be here when he could be at the county fair with a cold soda and a pet goldfish in his backpack?"

"We always reorient our patients."

"Ah. Well, in that case, I will do exactly that as soon as you leave the room. Thank you, doctor."

Not all of the doctors were like that. Most of them were incredible. The nurses even more so. The hospice team, angels. But there was something happening with the palliative team that rubbed Hal wrong from the get-go. And in the end, I understood why. While they were clearly the experts when it came to cancer and pain management, they did not know Hal. They were not with him while he was lucid. While he was healthy. While he was alive. This new version—vulnerable and open, plucking memories from a hat as his body shut down—was a different kind of man. A magical version I was finally, at the very end, getting to know.

For weeks, I sat in his audience and took notes. For weeks, I left his hospital room only for coffee in the mornings, afraid I would miss hearing a story from him or a sentence. So many of his words evaporated before I could gather them. Before I could pull them down from the hangers with both arms.

These, I wrote down:

It just grows and creates. It's like a well.

I said I love you on the night trip.

What time is it OH MY GOD THAT'S AMAZING.

Oh wow. She's been here more than a day.

I don't even know what is happening.

I have the single. And I'll perform it even if it isn't ready.

Should we turn around?

They're not doing anything. They're just waiting for the phone to ring.

When she came . . . I can't erase this right now.

I wouldn't lie to you. I would never lie.

I find the smaller moments so much more peaceful.

I came to the party because they all wanted me to be there and they were so supportive of the codes.

I don't know if that will continue tomorrow but I just wanted to tell you today.

I'll tell Archer and maybe he will?

Sometimes you don't know if there's going to be a shooter. It's all just part of your life, right?

Ask the girls if they want to watch the motorcycle racing.

I don't want to do it alone.

Do you think this will continue?

Bec. There's food waiting for you in the refrigerator downstairs. I think that's true.

Hold on a second this conversation is getting so unwieldy. I'm just trying to get advice from you. Am I on speaker phone?

Poor Becca.

Nobody is going to build that into the schedule quite yet. Is that correct?

I didn't realize the Black Panthers would be here tonight.

Sorry I ruined your Friday night, Bec.

Whatever you need to help me pull through I'll come and find you as soon as I can.

Let's not waste precious time to be on the road.

Oh wow, you're a patron saint.

Eat whatever you want. Go to the park. Life. Sneak. Snack. Lunch. Dinner. Learn about cooking.

Infinite choices with profound possibilities yes or no.

People love their air pods. They can't get enough. Mmmhmm, obsessed.

What happened? We're wrapping you up.

We got tickets last night for an advanced screening. I think it's the same theater.

They're covering the tombstone. They get no light.

He just sat there and healed. The microphone. It just sat there and got better.

You can easily learn about the illness. How it works how it attacks. You can easily learn about it in a day.

I never did the laundry last night. I never did it. I put it in here because

I thought there would be more to collect. I'm 99 percent sure I didn't start it. I'm sorry.

Rush has two new bands. One checks their covers at about 50 percent completion and the other one is kinda silly. It's called Fly Over something. They need a better band name.

What were we talking about? How to spoon? Ah. How to pour it into a glass so we can heat it.

I just finished. But we need to do more work on them. You see? Pray.

I was lucky. (smiles)

Okay then. Let's go.

They're getting delivered.

I haven't had ice water in two weeks. I'm gonna pour it all over my balls.

We all get hungry. I get it.

I've learned a lot about myself this past month.

Is this a spoon? A spoon that says I love you on it?

Think about using your goals. Your music. To better understand you. Don't make big judgments.

When things get harder just remember to breathe deeply.

I can't climb. I have to walk all the way around instead.

Do you have a pen? I need to write something down.

Close your eyes. Close your eyes. Close your eyes.

That's exactly how he said it, too. Three times in a row like he was singing a song.

When I think of Hal on his *deathbed*, which I suppose is what it was, I think of him smiling and nodding his head like someone somewhere was saying something funny, like he was being invited to life's after party. *Guest list only. I'm sorry, how do you spell your last name again? Okay, yes, you're in. But no plus ones. Only you can pass through the velvet curtain. Sorry, man. I don't make the rules.*

It was as if Hal was dipping a toe in the in-between so that he could prepare his whole body for its next episode. This is why I knew better than to reorient him. Why the hell would I pull the pen from his fingers mid-story? This was as close as I was ever going to get to closure. To hearing him unplug from his past so that he could connect to whatever was next. So he could release what he was still holding on to. So he could sleep and continue to live.

A few days before Hal stopped speaking and a week before he died, he had the most incredible hallucination of them all.

Fable had just been elected student body vice president of her elementary school. Her ability to stand on the podium and speak eloquently in front of the entire student body as her father lay dying was just one example of her fortitude, bravery, and grit.

Her teacher texted me as I sat with Hal in his hospital room: "Fable won. Landslide victory. It wasn't even close."

I had seen Fable's speech and was not surprised. I have a picture of her walking from the podium into the audience, a streak of crimson in her hair, chin up, eyes fixed on the camera's viewfinder: strength incarnate.

"We made amazing kids," I said to Hal, upon reading aloud the series of texts mainly intended for him. He nodded, his eyes still closed, barely registering the words I read to him.

I wasn't sure he could hear me, but I kept reading. Held up photos of our daughter, just in case.

Minutes later, Hal suddenly sat up. His eyes were wide, smile big, hands together, clasped as in prayer.

"Is this thing on?" he said tapping at an invisible microphone.

It's on.

"First, I just want to say thank you to everyone for coming today. I also want to thank you all for believing in me enough to ELECT ME STUDENT BODY VICE PRESIDENT!"

Hal threw his arms in the air just as his hospice nurse walked in. The two of us looked at each other and immediately starting clapping. Cheering. Inviting strangers from the hallway to do the same.

"It is my honor to represent you all. I promise, I won't let you down."

Tears ran down his cheeks.

"Congratulations!" I said. "I'm so proud of you. You did it!"

He held one hand against his heart and, bowing his head, pointed to the ceiling with the other.

"Thank you for believing in me," he said.

Lucidity is not the goal in death. Poetry is.

CHAPTER 8

The Last Sunset

Archer was born on the third floor of Cedars-Sinai thirteen years ago. I was twenty-three years old and you were thirty. I tore wide open when he was born but that was because the doctor cut me first. I was so afraid to give birth and he looked me dead in the eyes and said, "if I don't cut you, you will tear all the way down," so I cried and said yes. And then I watched the doctor disappear beneath my swollen abdomen, pushed when he said push.

"Like this?" I asked.

"Harder."

Birth is violent in a way I was wholly unprepared for, which explains a lot of things, actually. I was a pacifist before I understood that sometimes war is the only way to make room for new life. That pushing a child out into the world is the ultimate act of hope.

That morning, I clutched my screaming child to the breasts I was still self-conscious of. "Breasts aren't for feeding, they're for feeling up," I thought, which of course, isn't true. But in those days, I was so confused about where to separate the mother in me from the girl I was told I was, that I recoiled when I showed my nipple to the lactation specialist.

I never told you that, though. Probably because I felt ashamed. I wanted so badly to be taken seriously as a mother, especially in those first few hours. I was afraid that if the doctors knew the truth, they wouldn't let us take him home.

Sometimes, out of nowhere, you would talk about the morning we went from two people to three. You remembered so much more than I did about the birth. I was out of my body, I think, for most of the time. But there you always were with your perfect memory.

I do remember some of it. I remember whispering to Archer that I loved him. "Welcome to the mess," I told him. "Please forgive me if I don't know what I'm doing. I'm just a baby, too."

I didn't say those things in front of you, there were so many things I didn't know how to say in front of you. We were still so new to each other when we became parents to the same child.

I was embarrassed about the things I couldn't control, like, "please don't tell me there was shit coming out of me while I was giving birth." I covered your mouth before you could respond. I do remember that. And then you pulled my hand off your lips and told me it didn't matter. That you had never loved me more, and it was true. I knew it was true and, sometimes, when I wondered if this was all a mistake, I thought of you in that moment—all of the things that didn't matter. And how much I loved you, too.

"Look what we made together by accident . . ."

Archer's brand-new body looked nothing like I expected. I didn't know then that, at birth, almost all babies' eyes are blue. He looked like your dad when he was born. He looked like an ancient tree, his tiny bird body with a face like a grandfather clock. His eyes unable to blink. What are you looking at, little man? What do you see?

I had never seen you cry like that.

". . . can you believe?"

Our something new.

He was perfect, so in a way, it felt like we were, too. Strangers still, with *years to go before the cracks would give way. In that moment, though, one floor away from where we are right now, I don't think two people have ever loved each other more.*

The kids are allowed in his room now and Hal is unresponsive. I don't know what you call what is happening to his body. He's comatose. He cannot talk or blink or speak or swallow. He is a dead man with a pulse who, I am told, can still listen.

"Keep talking to him. He can hear you," I tell our children, but they just look at me cockeyed. How does a seven-year-old know what to say to a parent who can't respond?

"Hi, Daddy."

"I love you, Daddy."

"We're back, Daddy."

"We're here."

Everyone wants their words to come out like prose at the end of someone's life. Like flowers at a funeral. Perfectly white without brown spots. Six dozen roses coiffed to perfection spread all over the bed like a stock image on a hallmark card.

In the real picture, no one is talking. My son is looking at his phone, scrolling through Instagram, peering through the windows at kids his age who are doing something different than watching their fathers die.

The girls are noticeably bored. Our tragedy has become mundane. A small stuffed dog with a pink bow around its neck sits unmoved on Hal's left shoulder.

It is an incredibly normal thing to die. Surreal, sure, but only because we have convinced ourselves that our existence is more important than acknowledging our ephemera. Death makes people panic until they're living against it every day. Four months in and none of us could remember what "before" even looked like. How quickly we adapt in times of crisis. Fall into new roles. Abandon old lives. Sit bored on the edge of death beds scrolling our forefingers against our phones. Children are still children, and teenagers are still teenagers, and a hospital room is still a hospital room even when their dad is dying in it.

There is a nonchalance to waiting. It doesn't matter what it is we're waiting for. Perhaps that is why we are so afraid to die. Because, eventually, everyone will arrive at the same ledge. That's how death has always looked to me in my thoughts. Like the cover of Shel Silverstein's *Where the Sidewalk Ends*.

"EDGE, Keep Off!" the crooked sign says.

But, of course, no one can.

Existence is temporary. When I am dying, children will stand around me, bored out of their minds, too.

In the beginning, the kids painted pictures and friends and family sent flowers and crystals and letters for me to hang around the room. At the end, the flowers were too much. So were the WE LOVE YOU, DADDY signs. Sometimes it's easier to face death in a room with blank walls. The pain in knowing you will never watch your children grow up is bigger than almost any pain I can imagine. Perhaps it was easier for him not to think about that in the end. I didn't understand it then, but I do now.

———

The doctors move in and out of the room, their coats a blur of perfect white. The food is untouched.

"But he isn't eating anymore. Why do you keep bringing food if he isn't eating?"

They shrug like the question is irrelevant and pass me the menu.

"For tomorrow's meals."

I pick up the little eraserless pencil. There are no right answers to this multiple-choice test. It's all bad. Even the kosher menu. We've tried everything at least twice.

"If he doesn't eat it, you can," they say. "You need to eat, too."

So, I check off the same boxes Hal did last week when he was able to hold the pencil. Mashed potatoes and fruit cocktail with a side of matzo ball soup. It arrives later and I keep the lid over the plate just in case. Everything feels like *a just in case* now. What if he wakes up? What if he's hungry? What if he can swallow again and I've already eaten his dinner?

Please close the door behind you.

Hours pass. I wait for the food to get cold and then devour everything on the plate. I do not realize how hungry I am until I see myself in the reflection of the window—a grown woman shoveling food into her mouth like a toddler. The insatiable appetite of a woman eating for two.

Hal's last meal is a smoothie my friend Jasmine brings for me from the spot around the corner. Or maybe it was Polly. Or Veronika. So many friends and family with faces those last few days and I wish I knew who to credit for their generosity. Now I know why people have guest books at funerals—the indecipherability of it all.

I do remember the smoothie, though. It was purple.

"The most LA last meal of all time," Hal would have joked if he could speak.

He hasn't eaten in two days when he points to the smoothie in my hand. It is almost completely full and I am stunned by his wanting. He opens his mouth slightly as if to say yes and I hold the straw to his mouth. A room full of friends watch him drink in silence. No one dares make a sound. We are as still as statues and when he finishes, we all whisper *yessssssssssssss.*

Hours later he is unresponsive. Unable to swallow or speak or close his eyes.

The next day, the doctors try to give him chemo pills first thing in the morning when I am still asleep. I wake up to the sound of them talking to him, spring up in the same clothes I've worn for four straight days, and ask if we can talk in the hallway. I am furious and exhausted and shivering with rage. *Are you fucking kidding me right now?*

"He can't even swallow, and you want to give him pills?"

"It could give him some extra time," they explain. "A week. Maybe more . . ."

A week maybe more of WHAT? Of fucking WHAT?

"Why would you want to keep him alive in this condition? I don't understand."

"Sometimes families do," the doctor explains.

"For whom?"

"The children."

The kids weren't allowed to visit Hal's hospital room until hospice took over. There are too many immune-compromised people on the fourth floor. Everyone has cancer here. Children with their dirty hands and their dirty shoes and their loud voices are too much for the patients.

Hal knew the kids weren't allowed to visit him the first day he was admitted months ago, and I wonder if that's why he never wanted to go home. Not because he didn't love his children, but because he did.

The nurses place a butterfly over the door of the dying and that's when the children can come. The butterfly is blue and laminated and reminds me of something a teacher would tape onto a child's desk with their name on it on their first day of school. Every time I think about it, I feel the same way I did when Hal was first admitted, when I asked the nurses why some of the hospital rooms had butterflies on them, even though I already knew the answer.

On this floor, when you see healthy children walking through the halls, it's because they have a dying parent here. Children are walking reminders of grief on the fourth floor in Tower B.

As with everything else, Hal refused to talk to me about end-of-life planning.

"I can't think about that right now," he said. "Just stop."

I assumed he wanted to die at home when the time came. But it became increasingly clear that he needed too much care and even more quiet—something only a hospital could afford him. And then, on the last day he was responsive, after months of his insisting on staying in the hospital, he suddenly had an overwhelming desire to go home.

"Get me out of here! WHY ARE YOU MAKING ME STAY HERE?" he kept asking.

"This is normal," the nurses assured me, handing me the WHAT TO EXPECT WHEN YOU'RE EXPECTING DEATH packet I had already read through a dozen times.

Terminal restlessness is what it's called. I had to call for the nurses to help me hold him down so he wouldn't get out of bed.

"But don't you remember? You said . . ."

"I WANT TO GO HOME!"

But he couldn't, and I had to tell him that in front of our children. He would have to die here in this room.

"I'm so sorry. I'm so sorry. I'm so sorry."

———

I have spoken about The Death dozens of times at this point. And every time I do, a new story emerges from the ending of another. It would be possible to write an entire book of endings that become beginnings that eventually end—a day in the life of a circle ad infinitum.

The very first night we spent together on the fourth floor, I heard a harp outside of Hal's room. I was overcome with gratitude that such a thing existed and assumed that harpists regularly came and played for patients and their visitors in the halls. Hal was too sick to leave his bed that night, so I filmed the harpist playing and showed him the video on my phone. "Next time she's here I'll come see," he promised. I was overly excited by the thought of our future hospital concert date and he thought it was sweet and squeezed my hand. But she didn't come back. Not for the rest of July or August or even September. Hal was hospitalized more than half the time he was sick and the only night the harpist came was the very first one. But I played him harp music from my phone and regularly checked in with the nurses. They assured me she would be back at some point, but it was always on her terms and "you kind of just have to get lucky . . ."

And then, on the evening of October 26th, I heard the strumming of a harp coming from the hallway. *Finally.* I raced out of the room, explained to the harpist that she had been there on our first night in July. That my husband was too sick to leave his room that night and I had hoped she would come back someday—that once again, he was unable to leave his room. I told her he was unresponsive and likely didn't have much time left and her being there felt like a gift.

Maybe she was the sign that he had sent to me and this was his goodbye.

By this point, the harpist had taken me into her arms and was hugging me.

"Bring me to him," she said.

She rolled her harp behind me down the hall of the hospital and into the room with the butterfly on its door.

And then she played.

Hal died seven hours later.

Hal wanted quiet in the end. When he was still home, I'd put on old movies or he turned on something called the Slow Channel, where he watched hours of train rides through places like the Swiss Alps. He was on a trip around the world, he explained, dozing off through Iceland's Route One to the tune of Sigur Rós.

He didn't want to talk about his death after that initial conversation around the table. He didn't understand that he was dying and, in his final days, kept asking me why he was having so many visitors.

"Because people love you and they want to say goodbye."

"Where are they going?"

"You're dying," I told him.

"But what do you mean, *dying?*"

He did not want closure and was annoyed by those who did. How neatly wrapped we want our packages, don't we? No one says goodbye until the party's over. Otherwise, it's awkward, like signing a school yearbook a month into the school year or breaking up and still living together. Like still being alive when people are saying goodbye.

The deathbed came to symbolize an entry point to epiphanies and confessionals and all of the things we waited until now to say. But mostly, it felt like we were all talking in circles. That's what it felt like when he didn't respond.

But sometimes he did respond.

One day, knowing Hal would miss his fall band performance,

Archer recorded his class in the practice room so that he could share the music with his dad when he came home. He inserted one ear bud in Hal's ear, the other in his own. Hal smiled gently as tears streamed down his cheek, his slender fingers extending into the air, pulling on invisible strings to the beat of Archer's bass lines— the proudest father in the history of dads.

───

It was early evening when they told me it was time to hook up the morphine drip. He was comatose and unable to swallow. I told the nurses I was going to take him outside for his last sunset and they agreed to wait until we got back. I rolled his wheelchair toward the end of the garden and sat down next to him, my arm outstretched above me, clutching his hand.

Our kids were there and my parents and siblings, the girls' laughter distant, *squeals echoing*.

Even in the gardens of hospitals, all games of tag sound the same.

Archer soon sat down beside me, stayed by my side, held my other hand.

There's a photo my brother took of us in this moment. Archer's head is on my shoulder and I am leaning toward him—my son—and away from Hal.

"This was how it started," I told him. "This is what we looked like when we began."

"—"

"You were the best of both of us, then. You still are."

My son, the fetus, the infant, the baby, the boy. My son, the man. My husband, the man, the boy, the baby, the infant. My husband, the corpse.

It started just like this, with the three of us huddled together against the unknown. And it would end in the same way. Just the three of us, watching the light change. *You and your full circles, Bec.*

Shortly after midnight, I whispered all the things I could think of that a person would want to hear before they die. And then I pulled Hal's chest toward mine and squeezed, an embrace that reminded me of the first time we ever put our bodies next to each other. When the flesh said yes before the mouth did.

His eyes changed color at the end. From hazel green to a deep blue. I was reminded of our newborn children and how their eyes were all the same until they were different.

Death has a way of making even young men look old and brand new all at once. Ancient, like featherless baby birds.

A dead man lies on a bed in a room and we are alone. I loved this man once and then I hated him and then I loved him and then I hated him and then I loved him and then I hated him and then I loved him again, and then he died.

This was our love story.

"I'm trapped" was the last thing he said to me.

And now I can go home.

You died on the fourth floor of Cedars-Sinai hospital just after midnight on October 27, 2018. I was thirty-seven years old and you were forty-four. Your eyes were wide open even though the nurses tried to close them in the end. "Why must you close his eyes?" I asked when they repeatedly kept trying. "Perhaps he is looking at something he can still see . . ."

So they left the room and us alone, you with your wide-open eyes and the sheet they pulled over your swollen abdomen up to your chin.

Death is violent in a way I was wholly unprepared for, which explains a lot of things, actually. I was a fighter before I realized that peace, in the face of death, frames acquiescence with a sort of holiness. That acceptance while dying is far braver than resistance.

"He lost his battle," they often say when someone dies of cancer, a universally accepted ignorance that war is greater than its opposite. That an incurable disease is no less capable of miracles. That "keep fighting" is the opposite of "rest in peace."

I was a warrior before I told the doctors to stop trying to keep him alive with meds that didn't stand a chance. Before I realized that all miracles do not look the same.

The night I clutched you, barely breathing, to my chest, I was still self-conscious of our love. It was so hard for so long that I skipped back to the beginning and told you stories from memory of how it all began. You were the first person I ever watched die and I didn't know whether or not I was doing it right. It reminded me so much of becoming a new mother. How you're just expected to know what to do. How you always support the neck.

The nurses don't know our history, so when they see me lie with you, I hear them whisper, "Look how much they love each other," and even though it's true, I have never felt more like an imposter. I close my eyes and plead guilty. I dream of you smothering me with pillows in my sleep. I wake up and tell you how sorry I am that this is how your story ends.

I don't remember if I said any of those things out loud. I know I said I was sorry a thousand times and meant it more than any apology I have ever made. There were so many things I didn't know how to say in front of you. And I am sorry for that, too.

When the hospice nurse told me that hearing was the last sense to go, it made me afraid that I would say the wrong thing and you would die with *the inadequacy of my words in your ear. That whatever happened next might be tempered by an unfinished sentence or a word misunderstood.*

You believed in an afterlife—that you would be born again in a mother's arms so I did everything I could think of to prepare you for your birth. I told you that I loved you and I promised to take care of our children. To raise them with honesty, courage, and love. And then I promised to raise myself, too.

You can go now. Please don't worry. I am so strong because of you. Because of this. Because of us. My something old. Blue. Borrowed . . .

Everything is borrowed until it is free.

You are free now.

We are free now.

I am free.

Part Two

Part Two

CHAPTER 9

Green

Early on in Hal's illness, Bo draws a portrait of me. I am standing in the middle of a field surrounded by a red fence. My eyes are Crayola green—and wide open. They are also bloodshot, veins like lightning bolts connecting iris to eyelid.

She proudly presses the portrait to her chest. "It's you. See? Do you think it looks like you?"

"I do! Yes! Especially the eyes, ha! But, tell me . . . why is there a fence?"

"That's not a fence, those are flames. You are standing in the middle of a fire. But see your face? You're not afraid. That's because you know you're going to be okay."

CHAPTER 10

Still Life

The irony of claiming freedom in the moments after Hal's death is that it takes months before I know how to separate myself from his ghost. I continue to move through the next days and weeks and months wearing clothes with so many pockets—*this many* pockets—so that I can carry it all with me while I hold my children's hands.

When people die young, we get to finish their stories. We get to assume they would have changed at some point. Or we forget they even had flaws at all. In the beginning, I put aside all the things that made Hal human—the ways our relationship paralyzed me, how afraid I was to call him out. I loved him in the end the same way I loved him in the beginning, purely and unconditionally—selflessly. The way women do.

I do not belong anywhere on the other side of Hal's death. Not yet. No one knows what to say to me, but everyone is staring. I am trapped behind the kind of glass that looks like a mirror: where everyone can see me but I can't see them back. In this room I am surrounded by images. Which one is this, again? Ah, yes. Sock footage.

At Cedars-Sinai, the socks are bright yellow with white anti slip treads on the top and the bottom. There are no left and right feet here, only swollen ones. Hal's feet were so bloated at the end, he couldn't wear shoes, only the day-glo socks he wore through parking lots and down hallways. Yellow became dark gray became black, the color of asphalt, until we replaced them with a new pair, bright and sunny.

Hal died in those socks. They remained on his swollen feet until someone at the morgue removed them. I wasn't there for that part, but I can't stop picturing it. Did the swelling go down in the hours after he died? Or did they freeze his body like that? The fluid hardened under purple skin. Is that how it works? What if he wasn't dead after all? What if he was almost dead but not quite? What if he was trapped in a body that was suddenly freezing?

Stuck on this possibility, I do not sleep for several nights. I think of him in a refrigerator with cold feet and no socks. *Where did they put your socks?*

I wake up gasping for breath, imagining Hal alive and freezing and unable to die with ice cubes for feet. Cartoonish squares of lavender and powder blue.

I panic and call to expedite the shipment of his body so that they can cremate him sooner. Apparently, this is common. Like shipping a package—if you pay more money, they will prioritize the burning of human remains. How fucking weird is that? But at the time, it was absolutely worth it. Setting Hal's body on fire was far more palatable than imagining him with cold feet.

I prepare to drive my children to school on Monday morning, two days after Hal's death, because that's what they want. *Everything to feel normal again.* Because everyone is looking at them, too. Same mirrored glass.

And then there's this other part that takes me completely by surprise: *The kids are okay.* They're sad, of course, but they're also happy.

They laugh and throw Cheerios at each other in the back seat. They say MOMMMMMMM in the same way they always have. They hurl stage-combatesque punches at each other. Ask me to play their favorite songs.

This week it's "Bad Girls" by M.I.A.

Who's gonna stop me when I'm coming through?

What we got left is just me and you . . .

They ask me to turn it up and I do. I put the volume on full blast as we pass the hospital that houses the morgue with Hal's body—frozen and blue without socks.

Live fast die young bad girls do it well . . .

Our voices belt out the words in octaves I didn't even know we could reach.

Past tense was present tense was third person was first. I talked to him out loud in the car and in the shower and in my sleep. I told him secrets like he was a priest at a confessional, assuming he would find out anyway now that he was a ghost.

You, I said. *Do you hear me? Are you seeing this right now? Do I need to tell you what happened today, or do you already know?*

Sometimes I forgot he was dead, picking up my phone to fill him in on family moments. I even texted him multiple times in the days that followed his death only to feel the buzz of his phone in my own back pocket.

As we approach the school, "My Vag" by Awkwafina is blasting. I turn it all the way down so we look like every other gray minivan in the carpool line. Part of me wants to say fuck it. People are looking at us anyway. Might as well throw everyone off with a rap battle about vaginas, but the girls are trying to maintain a low profile and so am I.

I scrape my tires against the curb, throw the car into park, reach my hands into the backseat to say goodbye to my daughters. *My* daughters. *They are only mine now. How is that possible? How can that be?*

One of our elementary school's premiere doting dads is waiting for my fatherless daughters to step out of the car.

"Good morning, ladies!"

His voice is unusually chipper—understandably, as he is clearly trying to be kind and welcoming to three girls who no longer have a dad—but something about his Barney the Dinosaur tone makes me want to punch him in the jaw.

The girls look back at me with a sort of knowing glance. Like, can you believe this guy? They're so little, but they know so much more than they did four months ago. They're aware that this well-meaning dad is overcompensating because he feels sorry for them and when they reach their hands toward mine on the way out the sliding door, I don't let go right away.

"I love you!" I scream out the window.

"I love you, too, Mom."

I want to fall on my knees and throw my arms around my daughters for being so brave. For walking right past Barney without knocking his ass to the ground.

This is the first of many times my hands will become fists when I'm around other children's fathers. Is this what Elizabeth Kübler Ross meant when she drafted her five stages of grief, anger being the second stage? It has only been two days since Hal died. It is out of character, I think, for me to be this early.

Still Life #6781: I am in a diner meeting a friend for lunch when the waitress drops a white porcelain bowl between us. It is full of tiny plastic creamer packets with paper peel-off tops.

And just like that, I am back in the hospital. I am drinking coffee at 4 a.m. on a Tuesday, watching Hal's paralyzed silhouette in the window. I cannot look out into the darkness without seeing the outline of his face in the reflection—the sunken eyes and cheeks like wishbones and eyelashes so long they cast shadows. There are lights in the windows across the parking lot and I wonder who else is drinking cold coffee. I wait for someone to show up on the same floor in a different wing. But after four months of waiting, I lose hope for that kind of symmetry. Instead, I watch Hal's face, unmoving against the endless night.

The nurses bring me creamers by the handful, familiar with the way I take my coffee. No on the sugar. Yes on the cream. Two. Wait, three. *Fuck it, make it four.*

I accept them with open hands, like the recipient of a spiritual offering, and they fall through my fingers in slow motion. Roll under the hospital bed and stay there.

Remind me to look under the bed if I run out of cream.

Everywhere I go is another reminder of how out of place I feel. This is what it must be like to come back from war and try to live as a civilian. Everything feels so overwhelmingly bizarre. People care deeply about stupid shit and cry for no reason at all. Or they say things like, "I know it's nothing compared to what you're going through . . ." which is even worse.

I don't know where I belong right now—certainly not at restaurants. Certainly not in stop-and-drop lines in front of elementary schools full of people who don't know me but also definitely *know*. I order food off the menu but eat very little of it. The coffee, though. The coffee ... reminds me of cream under the bed.

———

Still Life #471920: The "Preparing for Death" pamphlet with a coffee stain on its front. I thought for sure I brought the pamphlet home from the hospital with me, but it turns out, no. I kept nothing to remind me of those last days. I didn't even take a picture of Hal after he was gone and I take pictures of everything. Always have. *I don't want to remember him like this*, I remember thinking. I didn't want the kids to someday find a picture of him dead, or a pamphlet with helpful tips for how to watch a young man die stained from their mother's coffee cup.

But I can't keep my children from the well-meaning words of near strangers.

"I'm sorry to hear of your father's passing."

"Are you okay?"

"I'm so sorry for your loss."

Loss. Father's passing ...

I have never used these words with my children. Neither did Hal.

"I will die," he had said to them on that first day and it was such a relief to hear him say it. To know that he wouldn't gloss the whole thing over and play Santa Claus. The kids deserved the whole truth. All children do.

———

Archer was the first one I told that Hal was dead. My parents were staying at my place, fast asleep on the couch when I came in through the door around 3 a.m.

Archer was awake. Couldn't sleep. *How could he possibly sleep?*

So I got into bed with him. Pressed my face into his back, and exhaled.

"Why are you home?" he whispered. But he already knew the answer.

We cried, of course, because it is impossible to tell a child his father is dead without tears. I told him from behind his back, my arms around his chest so I could touch his heart. Feel it beat beneath my hands. The life in him continuing.

"I love you. I am here now. I am here now. I am here."

We fell asleep like that, and in the morning, I woke up to Bo and Revie standing over us with the same question.

"Hi," I said. "Come here."

"He's not in pain anymore. Right, Mama?"

"Right."

And then we soaked our hair with each other's tears.

Hours later, I broke the news to Fable in the car outside her best friend's house. She insisted on sleeping there the night he died, knowing what was coming. She wanted the distraction. She needed the distraction. At her age, I would have wanted the same.

Of course you can do a sleepover.

But just like her sisters, she knew. The fact that I was there, parked outside in the van in the same clothes I had worn for the last week. She climbed into my lap and folded.

The kids had no desire to see grief counselors and, perhaps because I didn't either, I didn't push it. Instead, we did what we always did. We drew pictures and played music and lit candles and danced around the house with bare feet singing "Ring Around the Rosie." We did our own version of familial mourning. We made stuff and burned stuff and cried and laughed and made macabre jokes and decorated the house for Halloween with skeletons and a dozen freshly purchased gravestones. We shopped for plots in the cemetery while blasting haunted-house sound effects on our phones. We sang along to Hal's favorite songs. We danced in the middle of grocery aisles, life-sized plastic skeletons in our arms. We laughed until we cried until we cried until we laughed and *ashes, ashes, we all fall down.*

Still Life #8989893: The five of us being the kind of family Hal would have been so proud of. This becomes the nucleus of my grief—Hal's absence from even the most mundane of family moments. The fact that he was once part of this dance party and now he's not.

The day after Hal's death, Revie drew a picture of the remaining five of us gathered around Hal's grave at his "forty-sixth birthday party *two years ago in the future.*" In the picture, she is holding my hand and we are wearing matching HAL skirts. There's an arrow pointing to Hal's grave, which reads "HAL IS COOL," and every one of us is labeled along with our ages. Revie proudly shows it to me, excited to provide an illustrated manifestation of a future where even in death, we will motherfucking party. And had I drawn what I wanted us to look like two years ago in the future, it would have looked exactly the same.

Still Life #989894: The cupboard full of sick person food. Dried fruit for constipation. Prunes and apricots, mostly. None of which Hal would eat once they arrived.

There is chicken broth and box juices and fruit cocktail and Jello. There are cans of soda, most of them grape, stacked high in the garage. The first and last time we will have soda in the fridge. I stare at the boxes and the snack packs and the Coca-Cola indecisively. I don't want any of this stuff in my house but, also, how could I possibly throw it away? *What if he comes back*, I keep asking myself.

Shhhhh, I know, I know. But, like, what if . . .

And so I do nothing. I decide to keep it all. Wait for it to expire. Throw it away when it becomes the only option. In the meantime, I go cross-eyed staring at all the apple juice.

Hal and I used to make the kids school lunches together. But I soon realize that it's a lot faster for me to pack four lunches on my own. That it's faster to do *everything* on my own. Maybe because I am awake now. On the other side of a life I was once consumed with breaking out of. A life that broke all on its own.

CHAPTER 11

Ash and Bone

In the blue light of Hal's hospital room, moments after he was de-
clared dead, a woman appeared in the doorway. I had just called
Hal's parents who were on their way. When someone dies you only
get a handful of hours with the body, so even if it's 1 a.m., you have
to call. Wake people up. Tell them to hurry up and come.

"If you want to see the body. If you want to say goodbye . . ."

So when I heard the knock, I was expecting it to be Hal's family. Instead a small-bodied woman pushed open the door and introduced herself.

"I'm sorry for your loss. I'm with decedent affairs," she casually
announced, handing me her card. "Do you have plans for the body?"

Plans for the body. Plans for the body. Plans for the body. Those words
on repeat as I stared blankly in her direction and then back at Hal
in case he knew how to answer her. We had talked about death a
thousand times when we were married but only in the context of
what to do with our bodies if and when we died.

"Donate my organs if possible and then burn the rest of me in a
fire."

I knew that the combination of cancer and chemotherapy would make donating his organs nearly impossible, but I had read in the advanced care pamphlet that there *might* be a chance his corneas were salvageable.

Suddenly I was a used car salesman, presenting my dead husband's eyeballs to a stranger like, "Look at these bad boys. Aren't they beautiful? Good as new. So little mileage."

But she told me the cancer had taken everything. Even his eyes.

"Yes to cremation. We're going to bury the ashes in a cemetery. Most of them. And then we will . . ."

"Great. Okay. And who will be cremating his body?"

"Oh. Um. I will?"

"No, I mean . . . what crematorium?"

But I didn't plan that far in advance.

"Do you . . . have anyone to recommend?"

She handed me a list of crematoriums as I made a joke about making some calls tomorrow, checking Yelp for reviews.

I expected her to laugh a little but apparently checking Yelp for crematoriums was normal and I just needed to contact the morgue "in the next forty-eight hours" with a plan. It was a relief to talk to someone so nonchalant about dead bodies. She was all business, stoic, unemotional. She didn't try to hug me or ask me *how I was doing,* which means I didn't have to answer. The business of death is a comfort in that way.

———

Noelle at Hollywood Forever hands me a black cardboard box. It is much smaller than expected. *This is all that's left,* I think, pulling at the thick plastic coated on the inside with the sand of his bones. *There he is, but what if it isn't him? Knock, knock. Hal, is that you in there?*

I wonder how often ashes get mixed up. How easy it would be to confuse them. We all look the same when we are set on fire, embers cooling, until at room temperature we are swept into a bag, put into a box. We are all the same shade of dust.

I look for him against the plastic. He had discoloration in one of his teeth and maybe if I look hard enough, I will find it.

I look for some sign of the freckles on his arms. His fingers calloused from playing guitar. *His collarbone is here somewhere.* Kneecaps. His eye sockets. I become obsessed with breaking him down the way the flames have. I close my eyes and trace my memory over his bald head—the way his skull indented where it connected to his neck. The small of his back, his hip bones, ankles. *Head shoulders knees and toes. Knees and toes.*

"Would it be okay to separate some of these ashes?"

"Of course," Noelle says.

Hal didn't have any dying wishes. He didn't want to talk about any of the decisions the kids and I inevitably made on our own. Like whether or not we would bury his ashes or where. He didn't want to talk about his epitaph. I agonized over this as he was dying, but it ended up being such a gift for the kids. His memory would live on in their image. His epitaph would come from their choice.

Hal loved cemeteries as much as I did and whenever we would see one by the side of the road, we would call out to each other, "Look! It's where the dead people live!"

Sometimes we would get out of the car.

"Hi, dead people!" we would say.

"Hi, dead people!" the kids would repeat.

"I don't know why people are afraid of cemeteries."

"Right? Isn't it amazing that people do this to each other after we die? We turn them into memories we can visit. We write things on rocks so that people who never got to know them can do so now. We create gardens full of monuments and bury our loved ones next to each other so their dust can merge."

Burying his ashes in a cemetery the kids could visit was something they unanimously wanted and, in the end, I wanted the dying wishes he didn't have to come from his children. But I also felt the need to let him go in a more visceral way—to scatter his remains on the surface of something. Somewhere he could move away from. And in perpetuity, become.

I hand Noelle a jar my sister, Rachel, sent me when Hal was still alive. Originally, it had housed various talismans: crystals, feathers, sage. . . . I had hoped that their energy was as inviting as it could be to what was left of Hal's. Before Noelle filled it with ashes, she asked if I wanted to wrap it with something.

"Sometimes people have a hard time looking."

Not me. Why look away from the only thing we are certain of? Why pretend that we won't lose the people we love the most in our lives, that they won't lose us back? Death, for me, was never the tragedy it was for everyone else. More like an elbow in the road. To be alive is to possess a future corpse.

Someday, someone will turn a glass bottle in her hands with the same curiosity I have. And it will be what's left of me inside.

———

I went to more funerals in high school than I can remember. At least a dozen one year. Suicides. Car accidents. Drug overdoses. Accidental self-inflicted shootings. Hit and runs. Senior year, my boyfriend and I were the first people on the scene of a car accident in which a friend was driving and flipped his car, instantly killing a boy I also knew. I called the ambulance. The car was upside down, the dead boy's body inside.

When his parents showed up to identify him, I was still there. I couldn't leave. I didn't want to. I had to stay until it was over. I watched them cover the rear window with a sheet. Everyone was crying. No one knew what to say.

Months later, my boyfriend would lose his sister. A relapse after years of sobriety. I sat next to him at both funerals. We did not let go of each other's hands.

At nineteen, I found a dead body in the alley of the 3rd Street promenade. A woman had jumped to her death from the top of the parking garage. When I called 911, I was told the coroner was already on their way. But I couldn't leave her lying there alone so I stayed with her, studied the way her limbs had twisted upon landing. Waited until the body was covered by medical examiners and then went to work.

It didn't occur to me to go home. I spent an entire day setting up meetings for my boss after studying a woman's body flattened against the concrete. Perhaps I was in shock. Or maybe I was so desensitized to death at that point it stopped fazing me altogether.

———

I placed the jar of ashes in my canvas tote bag with the necessary paperwork I needed to transport "human remains" across state lines.

Once alone in my car, I inspected it, turning the jar over on its side and back against my steering wheel. I studied the dust like a word search, trying to decipher Hal's body in the hourglass. I loved his arms, specifically the skin near the armpit. That's where he was the softest. *The strongest parts of him were also the softest.* I imagined myself biting it. Like I did when we were fucking, or spooning, or falling asleep. Like I did when I couldn't keep my hands off of him and also my mouth. *Remember those early years where we used to salivate all over each other? Crisscross our DNA like shoelaces?*

I'm going to devour you. I am going to eat you alive. Swallow you whole. Lap up your sweat. Pull your hairs out with my teeth.

117

I explain this to the ashes I have remaining, inspecting his broken bones, imagining I am sucking the marrow from them like a wolf. Snorting his dust like lines of cocaine.

I imagine tearing his body apart like the fire, swallowing his freckles like a child sneaks cake sprinkles, *shake shake*, just like that into my open mouth.

I imagine consuming him in his entirety so I can keep what's left of his body warm in mine. Like I did for our children in my womb.

The number four emerged like a whack-a-mole during his four months from diagnosis to death. Stage four. Fourth floor. Age forty-four. Four children. His death falling four days before *Hal*loween— our favorite family holiday. Four as in the 4 in 143, pager code for I love you, the 4 = love. Reminding me of being young and signing off on folded notes to friends.

143—2—187, we would write.

I love you to death.

And so I plan for his service to be held on 11/11. (Make a wish.)

My friend April calls me with a brilliant idea to have Hal's service at The Whiskey a Go-Go, blocks from my children's school, and one of the most iconic musical venues in Los Angeles. They even offer to put Hal's name and dates on the marquee for no extra charge.

"Rest in power chords," it will say under his name.

They have never had a funeral at The Whiskey to the knowledge of the manager and I have no idea if we'll be able to pull this off, but my friends, who are magicians, come together and create the most exuberant, entertaining, life-filled memorial. They pack the room with chairs and candles. They make programs and simultaneously mastermind a catered after-party at our house. They work tirelessly and lovingly and create an event that defies expectations. They put the fun in funeral, and I don't know how I got so lucky for *these women* to be my team.

I am deliberate with my wardrobe—borderline unreasonably obsessed with finding the perfect dress to send a message I am unable to articulate from the podium.

I find a long black dress that screams afterlife. It's long enough to hit the floor but just barely, and down its middle curls a snake, its head resting sternly on my heart, eyes wide open, protective. A bouquet of multicolored peonies bloom down my legs, a trail of moths and butterflies in formation above a second snake, the exact mirror image of the first—a Rorschach test that nobody knows they're taking. A poem they can interpret as they wish.

I don't remember much about the funeral. I am barely cognizant when Archer, on keyboard, opens the service with Van Halen's "Jump."

I get up. And nothing gets me down.

I am somewhere that isn't my body for the speech I deliver in front of an audience of indecipherable faces.

You got it tough, I've seen the toughest around

I don't remember a single image from the slideshow Hal's friends and former coworkers create for the service.

And I know, baby, just how you feel

I know that my brother performs an original song. That our friend Toby does, too. I know that Hal's brother and his best friends from childhood tell stories I've never heard before. That my sister plays Debussy's "Reverie" on flute. The song that inspired the name of one of our daughters.

You got to ro-oh-oll with the punches to get to what's real . . .

The day Hal died, a turtle appeared on our driveway—the kind of turtle that cannot survive for very long without a pond. So how did it get there? How did it end up at our house, two blocks from the park where it likely started? I didn't have answers but the kids certainly did.

"It's Dad. He's letting us know that he safely crossed the road to get to the other side."

Children are magical thinkers. It's why they're so much better than adults are at death. I have navigated every day since Hal has died, not as the lighthouse, but as the ship that sails toward the four beams of light that are my children. They didn't just see a turtle. They never have.

The turtle became an instant symbol for Hal and our life without him. Turtles came up constantly after that. Friends and family filled our home with turtle imagery, cards, and jewelry. And when it came time to design a headstone for Hal, the kids drew up their own—a turtle.

The stars on the headstone separating the dates were copied directly from the star tattoos Hal had on his shoulder. Three little stars representing birth, death, and what comes after. The three tenses, like portions of hair in a braid. If death was a shape, it would be a triangle. If death was a satellite, it would be a star. *Do you feel it? Like an exploding ball of doom, but also hope.*

Archer suggested Hal's high school yearbook quote as the epitaph.

Thank you all for your time.
It has been incredible.
Anything can happen. Believe.

We will bury Hal's ashes the week before his service. Kind of like having a wedding in private and then a public reception. It felt right to do it this way—to give the children shovels and blast Hal's favorite album and have the kind of burial most adults would not understand. I think Hal would have wanted this, too. He, like me, didn't understand the stoicism of goodbyes. He would have wanted a dance party. He would have wanted *this*.

It was just the five of us and my friend Linda.

From the moment of Hal's diagnosis, Linda had been my death doula, holding on to my paperwork and making calls on my behalf. She was the one who organized the notary public to come to Hal's hospital room so he could sign the power of attorney documents. She was the one who reached out to his employer in the weeks after his death. Helped me with tax documents and insurance policies.

She was the one who called Noelle at Hollywood Forever to see if there were any available plots soon after Hal died. She organized the payments and payouts—went over documents so I didn't have to. Vetted everything. She was one of the many women in my life who made it possible for me to be the wife and mother I desperately wanted to be at the end. She also helped organize the burial. And so, after checking in with the kids to see how they felt about it, I asked her to join us.

On the day of Hal's burial, ash was falling from the sky like Purple Rain. It was early November when we found ourselves reluctantly nestled under a blanket of smoke, arms linked as we trekked across the expanse of newly mowed grass and granite toward a tent we didn't realize was erected in our honor, cerulean against a chestnut sky.

"Is that tent for us?"

"Yes."

"But it's only us."

"Yes."

The weather hadn't changed much since early July when Hal was first diagnosed. Here we were, months later, and the fires were still blazing uncontained in the hills. But the smoke provided a kind of privacy we might not have had otherwise. We would be able to dance around his grave with no one around us.

And that is what we did. What *they* did. His four perfect children, aged seven and seven, ten, and thirteen. All taking turns with the shovel. One at a time, throwing dirt on the box in the ground that was their father.

Dearly beloved. We are gathered here today
To get through this thing called life . . .

"Turn it up, Mama. This is the part of the song where we dance . . ."

CHAPTER 12

Coastlines

I knew from the beginning that we wouldn't bury all of him.

As much as the kids needed a place to visit, we also needed to release him into the wild. Most people put the ashes of their loved ones somewhere with significance—a place that held great meaning to the deceased—but Hal never talked about the places he loved, only the ones he wanted to see next.

Nostalgia didn't interest him. The future was far more attractive to him than the past and he spoke of tomorrow with the same wistfulness I reserved for yesterdays. What a strange paradox: the remains of a man who loved a future he would never experience in the hands of a wife incapable of making plans.

In one of my earliest text exchanges with Hal, he spoke of one day moving us to the Pacific Northwest. He told me he dreamt of living there. In a house overlooking the sea, where the fog was thick and the ocean was too cold to swim in. We talked about vacationing there as a family on multiple occasions but never actually took the trip. For as long as I'd known Hal, he'd dreamt of the Oregon coast. Now, for as long as there was an Oregon coast, it would dream about him back.

After Hal died, the kids came to me separately and asked if he had left them anything. I had been afraid this would happen but had hoped it was merely projection—that maybe I had seen one too many Super Bowl ads depicting dying dads and their prerecorded birthday messages for their surviving children.

Happy sixteenth birthday, son. Here's a tire-changing tutorial video I filmed for you while I was dying of cancer. I'm sorry I can't be there to teach you with my own two oil-stained hands, son, but would ya do yer old man a favor? Would ya tell yer mom I love her and ask for the keys to the Chevrolet? That's right, boy. Now that you're sixteen, the El Dorado is yours. I want you to drive her with the same pride I did. Into the sunset, son. That's right. Make me proud.

Annnnnd fade to black. *Chevy Runs Deep.*

But it wasn't just me who was hoping Hal would leave something for his children. Friends had come to me from the beginning, volunteering their camera equipment and production services to record messages for the kids to watch someday.

Hal couldn't do it and he didn't have to and I understood. Sort of. I understand more now, with some distance. I have let go of what I felt could have been a better death, accepting the complications that come with such mortal procedures. And while Archer took matters into his own hands when it came to the closure he had with his father, the girls were unable to ever really say goodbye—something I knew I would need to be proactive in helping them work through. The burial and funeral were important first steps, but I felt it was just as necessary for us to take a trip to a place that was equally unfamiliar to all of us.

What does it look like, not to start over, but to begin again?

I was desperate to sit alone, just the five of us, in a strange little house without the distractions of friends and neighbors. To create a point of entry where we could peel off from outer influences and become new—an intentional reframing of our lives. Like taking a honeymoon after a wedding, it was time for us to learn how to be a new way. Fatherless. Husbandless. Us.

The first place I found on Airbnb was in a little town called Arch Cape just south of Cannon Beach on the central Oregon coast. The house was tiny—a well-maintained shanty—located right on the water. It was as gray as the sea, with three fireplaces and one bedroom and a large couch that wrapped around a table overflowing with board games. Outside was a pathway made of rock and shells that snaked through a garden and a doorless entryway carved from twisted driftwood. The ocean was cold and rough and, since it was late November, we all had to bundle up to go outside. All of us except Bo, who, every morning, ran to the ocean in her underwear, wild-haired and barefoot, her cartwheels leaving handprints along the sand until the tide came up to collect them.

I gave everyone their own vial of ash and set them free to explore the beach on private memorial missions. They sprinkled most of the ashes in creeks and river mouths, above waterfalls, and on shorelines at low tide.

Bo was the last to empty her vial, choosing to climb to the highest point of the bluff where one waterfall pooled before becoming another. I watched her deftly balance with one hand, careful not to spill. Even as it became increasingly clear that it was only a matter of time before . . .

She tripped, the ashes a plume of smoke in the air above her. After a moment of silence, she looked back at me and screamed.

"Help me! Daddy is in my hair! DADDY IS IN MY HAIR!"

And then she cried. It was the first time since Hal died that she cried like that. It was deep, like thunder, an emotional sonic boom. I ran up the side of the mountain in rubber boots, my hands clawing the side of the bluff. *I'm coming I'm coming* I said, until I was there, and she was in my arms, collapsed against the chest of my coat, ash smeared with tears across her cheek.

"Look. It's almost gone," she said weeping, her hand tight around the near-empty vial.

It's hard to collect lost ash on a mountain. I had watched it fall upwards, vanish like smoke. I collected what I could from where I was seated but it was mostly just sand.

I told her that maybe this is where he wanted to be. *I mean, would you look at this view?*

Below us the tides were dancing, their waves rhythmic against the rocks. A line of pelicans lowered their beaks to meet their reflective twins. Way out past the break was an island that changed sizes depending on the highs of tide and the lows of coastal fog.

We watched in silence for a minute before Bo peeled away from my arms. She was better now, she told me, catching her breath, sprinting ahead.

"Come on, Mama. Let's go," she said. "There are still some ashes left."

Grief is nonlinear. It's sneaky and sharp, like a serial killer in a movie where there's no warning. No suspenseful music. No screeching of violins. And one night, when you think you're fine and everything is fine and *oh, look at me living my life*—thriving, even—it's like, BOOM BANG, then suddenly you're on the floor with no memory of how you got there. Grief put a roofie in your drink and now the room is spinning. Grief is supposed to be a Mack truck but, really, it's a Prius with its lights off. No way to know it's coming until you are under its wheels.

In those first weeks after Hal's death, I learned to welcome the tread. I knew the undoing always led to a more heightened awareness. Like being possessed by my own knowing. An exorcism I must have forgotten I signed up for. Like, *girl, I know you're*

in Trader Joe's trying to decide which pasta to buy but hear me out.
You need this.

There is something godlike about these moments of release, the irrefutable power of a seizure-like breakdown that ends in holy silence—the falling apart a catalyst for rearrangement.

We find new ways to open ourselves to change. This is our privilege. Evolution can only happen when bodies adjust to high tides and weather patterns and an earth that will not conform. No one can be the rock all the time. *Sometimes you have to let yourself break all the way down. Become the sand.*

Come on, Mama. Let's go.

———

To the left of our little house were rocks and a small cove, which appeared only briefly at low tide. On our first day exploring, a family staying nearby pointed it out to us. Their teenaged children had just come in from the southern direction, where the rocks jutted out and then broke away, boulders scattered like stepping-stones between the mainland and an island impossible to access because of the steep flatness of the rock.

"If you climb around those rocks, there is a cove under a giant archway," they told me. "Might be fun for the kids to explore."

Archway. As in Arch Cape. Of course. OF COURSE!

"Anyone want to check it out?"

Archer did. I made some dumb attempt at a "just like your name!" zinger to which he rolled his eyes. I told him to trade shoes with me so his socks didn't get wet. His feet were already bigger than mine, but he squeezed his feet into my knee-high Hunter boots anyway and ventured toward the archways. Within seconds he disappeared, obscured by the rocks and also what appeared to be a quickly rising tide. After what felt like several minutes, I began to panic. My panic quickly turned into desperation. Moments later, I was standing ankle deep in ocean, screaming out his name.

I was wholeheartedly convinced he had fallen off a rock and was, at the precise moment I was screaming his name, drowning. Dying. Dead. My fear of leaving the girls alone and possibly dying myself while rescuing turned into a three-headed monster of panic, anxiety, and fear that I would never be able to fully parent, protect, and comfort four children at once.

I was screaming for Archer, the girls were screaming for me, and we were all going to die—Archer from drowning, me from trying to save him, and the girls from being left alone on a remote beach in Oregon. The truth was, my panic had instigated theirs and pretty soon we were all standing, hysterical, shoes soaked in ocean, screaming into the void.

A couple who were walking their dogs came running to us.

"What happened? Are you okay?"

"My son is out there somewhere. Past the bend. He went to find the cove and hasn't come back."

The man quickly handed over his dog leash and went sloshing in the direction Archer had disappeared, returning moments later with an absolutely unscathed thirteen-year-old boy.

Archer, it turned out, had been very happily exploring, oblivious to our hysteria. He looked at us and mouthed the words "what the fuck" as I collapsed on the sand hyperventilating.

I thanked the man profusely, suddenly feeling self-conscious of my VERY apparent overreaction. It was so unlike me and I immediately felt ashamed. *I'm not usually like this*, I wanted to tell him. *I'm usually super fucking chill no worries it's all good like totally for sure.*

But oh my god what if it wasn't ... WHAT IF IT DID NOT TURN OUT TO BE CHILL?

Archer estimated he was gone for five minutes at the most, but to me it had felt like hours. The tide had not changed even slightly though I could have sworn on every one of our lives that it had. I had created a story in my head that was so convincing, I began to see the waves become menacing and the rocks become deadly. I had imagined one of my boots floating to shore and Archer face down, being pulled deep into the sea.

The truth is, the man didn't save Archer's life at all, but he quite possibly saved mine. Had he not showed up, I would have certainly gone looking for Archer, dangerously hysterical, with three little girls refusing to wait on the beach alone.

"Come on, Mama. Let's go."

I recall being well into my second trimester with Bo and Revie when Fable, at two years old, fell backwards into the Jacuzzi with her clothes on. I flung my body in after her so quickly I banged my pregnant belly on the cement going in. My instinct to save her was so strong that I forgot about my own body, which, at the time, included my unborn children. We all turned out okay, but for two seconds I didn't deliberate, prioritize, or think of anything but Fable.

Now it was different. My instincts were colliding—contradictory and indecisive—paralyzed by fears that measured equally. If I went after one, what would happen to the other three who were already going after me, knee deep in the ocean? It would be impossible to save myself. And him. And them.

Death was so central to our lives now. It was so close I could feel it nestled around us while we were sleeping. I could smell it on the breath of my kids when they screamed. I could feel it in the vulnerability of every heartbeat. There was nothing I could do for Hal, which woke me up to the realization that there was nothing I could do for my children, either. Every exploration was a risk. I had spent their entire lives, up to this point, unfazed by their use of knives and their desire to climb trees to the very top. I don't think I ever used words like "be careful" or "watch out." If anything, I pushed them to be more daring.

"A little blood won't kill you. Let me know if it doesn't clot."

Suddenly, it was overwhelmingly clear to me how easily I could lose one of them, or all of them, or myself. There were four of them and only one of me. Only one of me. Only one.

For the rest of the trip, we stayed together. If one person went down to the beach, we all followed. I peed with the bathroom door open. And at night, I slept with all four kids in my bed.

At the time, I assumed they had crawled in beside me as a comfort to themselves, but looking back I think maybe it was for me. Like they collectively knew I needed to be close to them. That I wouldn't have been able to sleep otherwise.

———

Several months after we spread Hal's ashes in the ocean, we took a trip to San Diego to spend some time with my parents for spring break. From the upper gardens of The Self Realization Fellowship, a botanical garden overlooking Swami's Beach, Revie pointed toward the ocean and asked if I thought *Dad was in there somewhere.*

"I do," I said. "What do you think?"

She thought for a moment and then nodded. "See those sparkles down there? I think that the sparkles are all the daddies and the ma-

mas and the children who die and are now in the sea. They're waving at us with the light . . ."

Revie took my hand in one of hers and waved back at her dad with the other.

This is why we put our loved ones in the sea. There is a calling here. There is an explanation. The most infinite expanse we can touch and feel with human fingers is the ocean.

"Come on, Mama. Let's wave."

CHAPTER 13

La Petite Mort

Le petit mort is French for "the little death," meaning "the brief loss or weakening of consciousness," and in modern usage refers specifically to "the sensation of post orgasm as likened to death." The peaceful afterward of post-release. The panting. The exhale. The bliss.

I think of this term often in the post-death weeks—how our most corporeal responses have a way of twisting their roots around one another. That it only makes sense for grief to trigger urges that are at once carnal, salacious, animal. That what I was feeling was probably extremely common in the wild. Chemical, even. But here? Where we measure our experiences against society's binary expectations for our domesticated lives, *How dare I feel such things?*

And while it made perfect sense to me in secret, I was still afraid to speak the truth out loud: that the moment Hal's life force left his body, I immediately became possessed by my own.

———

There are many support groups for widows, but I don't go to any of them. I would feel like an imposter showing up. What would people say if they knew that it's been weeks since my husband's death and I have never in my life felt more alive? What would they think if they knew that my heartbreak is nothing compared to my wanton need to get fucked? That the reason I burst into tears when people ask me how I'm doing is because I can't answer them. Not honestly.

Instead, I allow myself to feel my relief in secret and perform for the public like I always have. I tell the story that everyone wants to hear—a story that is so expected of me I know exactly how to tell it.

I know how to tell it so well that I wonder if, over time, I will start to believe it. That if I tell the whole world how sad I am that my husband is dead they will think that I am good. The kind of wife they hoped I was all along. The kind of widow that does right by her man by showing him nothing but love and sadness in the aftermath of his life. *I know how to say all the right things, so here, let me say them to you. Let me break all the way down and let you believe what you want to believe about why.*

I know that, in time, people will stop expecting me to grieve on command.

Just a few more months of this and I'm free.

Just a few more months and

I'm

free.

It doesn't even feel sexual, the yearning. It's more of a rumbling from deep within. The sudden recognition of an emptiness that was there for years—ignored, deprived, unsatiated. Like how you don't know you're hungry until you're suddenly starving. *If I don't eat now I will die.*

I am lying in bed, staring at the sky of the ceiling, thoughts fixated on what to call myself when introducing myself to a future lover.

Not that I would ever seriously use the word "lover."

Fuck buddy?

I am lying in bed staring at the sky of the ceiling, thoughts fixated on what I would call myself when introducing myself to a future *fuck buddy.*

No. That's even worse. I'm thirty-seven years old. A mother with four children. Women like me do not have fuck buddies. Women like me. Women like me. Women like me . . .

I don't know any women like me. *Hello? Are you out there? Can you hear me?*

I need a word for the way it feels to be newly widowed from a man I wanted to divorce. A man I loved but also hated. A man who, for the two years before he died, I barely touched. And while part of me feels it's desperately necessary to describe in detail all the ways Hal broke me, there is another part of me that forbids it. He's dead and I still feel the need to protect him. At first, I assume it's because I want to protect my children, but there is so little written in this book that they don't already know. They were here, too. They lived in the same house with the same man incapable of discretion when it came to rage.

No. This is me being at odds with myself. I have, up until now, been tender with my husband's reputation. I have said all the right things about all the moments I felt wronged. I have done his PR for free. Now I am possessed by the girl I was before we fell in love— who feels as though she's escaped into an open wood, desperate to tell the whole truth, like this is what she was waiting for all along . . .

No one can know.

But . . .

It isn't their business.

But...

He's dead now. Move on.

But is it possible to move on without first moving through? This is the part of being a widow no one wants to talk about, the part that has made me feel more alone than anything. It doesn't matter how much fun we had together. How funny and clever and brilliant he was. He made me feel crazy. He made me feel unsafe. He made me feel like a child who couldn't wait to turn eighteen and move out. He made me feel paralyzed: pretending to be asleep like I did the first time a boy touched me without my consent.

"You're such a heavy sleeper," he would say to me at the breakfast table the next day, and I knew exactly what he meant.

My first pregnancy was a direct result of Hal's refusal to wear condoms and his assurance that he would pull out—"no it's fine—don't worry—you have to trust me. I don't do condoms. No, seriously. I don't."

I understood his reluctance. I hated them, too, but I hated the idea of chlamydia and pregnancy more so I carried them with me everywhere and offered them to all the men who "had just run out." (They always seemed to just run out.) I was on the pill, but only sort of. Would forget more than I would remember, then take two pills every other day. I was reckless but I did everything (mostly) right in the aftermath of questionable situations—like taking my monthly pilgrimage to Out of the Closet, a thrift store on Sunset that tested for STIs and STDs. On a few occasions, because of broken condoms or hazy sexual encounters, I hit up Planned Parenthood for morning-after pills, washing them down with a hot cup of Starbucks on my way to Runyan Canyon. I was a casual kind of responsible. Nonchalant in emergencies. All peace signs and no worries, dudes.

I never faulted men for not wanting to use condoms. *Boys will be boys*, after all. Of course, it doesn't take long for a young woman to learn that a man who refuses to wear a condom doesn't care much about her future. In fact, he isn't thinking about it at all.

I knew all of this, and yet, with Hal, it was a different story. He was adamant about condom-free sex. And after the first few times we fucked, he removed them from the equation altogether. But instead of leaving instantly after I realized he had removed the condom without my consent, I stayed.

After all, he had never gotten anyone pregnant before.

"But what if . . ."

"You have to trust me."

"Can we just use them tonight?"

"No."

"You're an asshole, you know that?"

"Yup."

And he was an asshole, even then. He was an asshole from the day we met to the day he died. But in those early days and weeks and months, he could fuck me the way no one had before—the kind of sex that erases everything else. He quickly became the kind of drug worth dying for and, at the time, I would have risked everything to lie naked with him, panting in a heap of bodies, barrier free. Which is exactly what we did.

My plan was to get a new type of birth control, but by the time my appointment came around, I was already seven-weeks pregnant.

For years, I told myself the same story. We were both dumb kids who didn't know any better. How could it possibly be a mistake when our son was so perfect? My pregnancy was a miracle. It didn't matter how it happened.

After that, unless we were trying to get pregnant again, I always had an IUD. But none of them agreed with me. No hormonal birth control did. My hair fell out. I swelled, bloated. My periods either disappeared or became three times heavier. But I knew it was up to me to keep from getting pregnant. Bleeding through my sheets every three weeks was a bullet I would have to bite because, much like refusing to wear condoms, Hal refused to get a vasectomy. We fought about it, of course. I was a mother of four, who had been through three pregnancies by the time she was thirty. My body was thrashed and birth control didn't agree with me. The least he could do for me—for us—was that one thing.

But he wouldn't do it. He didn't want to. He could not spend one afternoon getting a minor procedure. And there was nothing I could do but say okay. I could take the suffering because I was the stronger one. That was how I justified it to myself. I could take years of heavy bleeding and hair loss, cramping, bloating, childbirth.

"Oh, you know. He doesn't want to, and I respect that. I mean. His body his choice, right? Right."

Keep twisting. Keep telling the story you want to believe. Stand by your man. One day, maybe he'll change his mind. Who are you to tell him what to do?

Then the 2016 election happened.

———

The night Trump was elected, I had a panic attack. We were at a party when my friend sat me outside with a bag to breathe into. *I think I need to go to the hospital.* I felt like I was going to die. It wasn't just Trump. It was me, too. It was Hal. It was a world of women being eaten alive by men who were repeatedly knighted in spite of bad behavior—women standing by their partners, their femininity a shield for men to be toxic behind.

The patriarchy was so convincing that even women—bleeding

and limbless, gagged with smiles safety-pinned to their faces— believed it was just.

I thought about all the times I defended men, even against my own best interests. Answering doorbells at 4 a.m. saying, *sure . . . but make it quick.* How I approved the friend request of a former friend who one night, during a movie, decided to pin me down on my own couch and jerk off on my face. How we never spoke again after that but that didn't stop him from commenting on my posts while Hal was dying. *Just another nice guy offering support.*

If I had a dollar for all the times I should have told them to fuck off, but didn't want to be a bitch . . . All the times I apologized for the blood. The mess. My womanness.

Suddenly, all I could think about was that our marriage, our family, our every joy was built on a foundation of rape culture, patriarchy, and a complete disregard for my body, feelings, and future. *I was a child who didn't know any better. He was a dude, so neither did he.*

I became obsessed with the cultural conversation that was happening around me. But how could I tell my story without hurting the people I love? It was impossible.

You cannot tell the truth without hurting people.

Suddenly everything I had written off as *okay* was being recognized for what it was: assault, abuse, coercion. It wasn't okay for a friend's older brother to molest me in my sleep when I was twelve. It wasn't okay to go on what was supposed to be an innocent walk in the woods only to be slammed against a picnic table, my "virginity" stolen from me under a blanket of stars. When you are used to being treated a certain way, it is hard to know what is and isn't wrong. And besides, wasn't I protecting myself by keeping the men in my life pacified? If I just let them . . . they wouldn't be angry or feel hurt or embarrassed. If I said yes instead of no, I could just leave when it was over and never come back.

So why did I come back? Why did I marry the kind of man I

would have told a million wives to leave? Why did I continue to have children with a man who made me feel like I was worthless? Why is that the person I believed I deserved?

I didn't tell anyone about these instances. Instead, I was obtuse about our marital struggles. Made light of it. *Live love laugh. Marriage, am I right?*

"Just breathe into this bag. That's it. Breathe in. Breathe out. Breathe in. Breathe out."

Breathe out. Breathe out. Breathe out.

It is impossible to write about sexual violence with nuance, but I've tried. I've forgiven rapists—mine and others. I've accepted apologies and moved on from much of the trauma I experienced long before I met Hal.

In writing about the complexities of past and present experiences, I was attacked from both sides. Blamed for my own assaults while being called out for forgiving them. I became obsessed with the root of the problem as opposed to the men who were upholding it. It became the soul of every essay I wrote. Every project I worked on. Every conversation I had. Because of my history, yes. But also because of what was happening in my own home.

———

Soon after the election, as I was sorting through memories and editing all of the stories I worked so hard to tell myself, I snapped.

I pointed my fingers in his face and listed every instance he did something with or to my body without my consent. For years, I woke up to him inside me, opened my eyes and stared blankly at the wall until he finished, rocking back and forth like an empty canoe. He would roll over after while I stayed awake, sticky against the sheets until the discomfort became too much and I had to climb out of bed to clean myself in the bathroom. Two hours later, I was there, again, in the same bathroom, shadows tucked neatly beneath my eyes. Voice like an alarm reminding my kids to get up, get ready for school.

I screamed at him with these and other stories in my mouth, convinced he had done the same shit to other women before we met. I was convinced that they would call him out and everyone would know I was the kind of woman who permitted the same behavior I spoke out against every day on social media.

He listened to me calmly, much to my surprise. He apologized, swore he was never like that with other women, even went so far as to reach out to ex-girlfriends for confirmation. He was like every other man I knew who grew up watching *Revenge of the Nerds* and *Sixteen Candles*. Who was taught that, by the very nature of being male, his pleasure was more important than my comfort.

And he was so sorry now.

I sobbed as he apologized.

"Why didn't you say no? You should have stopped me! I didn't think you cared!"

"Why would you want to fuck someone who *didn't care*!?"

I grew up listening to the adults in the room joke about "happy wife, happy life!" as if women were too demanding. The bare minimum can feel like that when you're a man who finds compromise daunting. It took me years to realize that *happy wife, happy life* was just another bullshit way to gaslight women into thinking their happiness was a punchline. *Happy husband, happy life* is more fucking like it.

I built a wall of pillows between us after that. And then I refused to have sex with him ever again. *Don't touch me,* I whispered if he tried. I hated him so much I fantasized about him falling off a cliff. Sometimes I imagined pushing him.

Then the diagnosis happened. I tore down the pillow wall the night he called from the hospital. I went from secretly wanting him to die to wishing I could rewrite our story so that we could both live without casting each other as villains.

So that when I told *the truth* about this—about us—no one would get hurt.

———

Perhaps it should not have come as such a surprise, that the moment Hal died, I opened up again. The moment his life force left his body, I felt something happen to mine. Something was stirring in me. Almost everything I was feeling felt impossible to say out loud.

I was angry.

I was relieved.

I was turned on.

People would bring me books about grief and how to heal and I flipped through them and felt worse. I did not see myself in any of these women. I did not believe that they were telling the whole truth about their marriages. Surely, they weren't this perfect.

I felt like a monster. A pervert. A sociopath. I wanted to be touched. Tenderly. By someone who understood how complicated everything was. I wanted to smoke post-coital cigarettes in someone else's king-sized bed while saying, "that was amazing."

I wanted to get fucked. Very fucked. Extremely fucked. On my terms—my pleasure, a priority this time.

I fantasized about all of the things I never asked for. Overnighted myself sex toys. Locked my door. I felt as if I was rediscovering my body. *Just the two of us—me and me.* But it wasn't enough. I wanted someone. But who would want me back? How could anyone respect a woman rebounding this fast from her husband's death? The father of her children! Her partner of fourteen-plus years!

I googled the feelings I was having and found only a handful of articles about dating "too soon" after death. I scoured the comments sections.

"Her husband just rolled over in his grave."

"She sounds like a real piece of work."

"She's disgusting."

"Her poor children."

I closed my computer and turned toward Hal's side of the bed. Imagined he was lying there. Watching me: a real piece of work.

———

There's a scene in *High Fidelity* where, the night of her father's wake, Laura (Iben Hjejle) decides to go after her ex-boyfriend Rob (John Cusack), who has just offered his sincere condolences. Laura watches him leave, and then, assessing herself in the mirror, gets an idea. She pulls her hair down, purses her lips, and takes off out the door, her blonde hair wild and unleashed behind her. Cut to a drenched version of the same seductress. She is now soaked in rain, in grief, yes, but also something else. Something intrinsically tied to her trauma—a want—no, need—to fill herself with something besides pain. And so, she climbs onto Rob's lap, hikes up her skirt, and proceeds to ride him into a new state of mind.

"Because I want to feel something else than this," she says.

There is no romance to this act. No love. She has come to him like a starving animal. So he feeds her. She looks down upon him as she takes what she wants.

I think about that scene constantly, the way she consumes him with open eyes. I wonder if the way I feel is not so different than the millions of women through time who have been through the same experience.

How does one feel alive in the aftermath of such a profound death? My body was crawling with answers that seemed to question every societal teacher. Every cell in my body was writhing.

I want to feel something else than this.

The opposite of *go* is *come*.

CHAPTER 14

Some Other Beginning's End

Soon after Hal dies, we lose power. It is the first minor crisis to avert as a solo parent and I welcome it as a challenge—like, *okay, you want to dance, energy department? Let's fucking dance.* It feels like a relief to be back here in the chaos. So as the kids stomp their feet in frustration, I prep for a night of adventure and the kind of lo-fi entertainment we could all use more of.

"Who wants to go candle digging! No one? You sure? It's really fun!"

The kids roll their eyes and groan as I rejoice in the discovery of an unopened box of Ikea tea lights and a stash of pillar candles left over from the funeral.

I set them up one by one on elevated surfaces as I'm pelted with questions.

When will this be over?

Will the power come back tonight?

But what will we do without computers? And cable? My phone's about to die and . . .

"I don't know," I tell them, which is my answer to most things these days.

I cannot and will not pretend that everything will be okay because there is always a chance that it won't—that we will live in a state of perpetual darkness against which we must make light.

———

In the weeks after Hal's death, everything in the house began to break starting with the roof above Archer's bedroom. In the past, I would have left it to Hal. Like I did when the smoke alarms went off because of low batteries or the toilet when it wouldn't flush. Now it was my turn to stop the water. The poetry of leaking ceilings was so obvious I had to marvel at the challenge of offering our home a Kleenex and a shoulder to cry on. I taped up the leak with layer upon layer of duct tape that I assumed would, at the very least, keep the water back for the night. LA rains are pretty tame, for the most part. But the duct tape wouldn't hold. Instead, it sagged until it burst.

"IT'S NOT WORKING! MOM! MOMMMMMM!"

"Cool, yeah, okay. Give me a sec. I'll figure it out."

Because I will.

I will stand in a room surrounded by broken things in a broken life with absolutely no plan whatsoever. I will experiment with home repair by attaching an open trash bag under the leak with a series of nails. And then by some HGTV miracle, my questionably executed contraption will catch all of the leaking water. Every drop. And in all my glory I shall crown myself the MacGyver of 3 a.m. roof leaks, because hear this, kids: *Sometimes "figuring it out" doesn't have to mean forever. It only has to mean for now—for the night. And then in the morning you can call the landlord.*

———

After the candles are in position, their tiny fires dancing in the early evening dusk, I decide to take advantage of our 90s music video inspired candle display and fetch my guitar. I am not good at guitar, although I did invest in a block of lessons in my early twenties. A friend of a friend had a studio in Encino that smelled like burps and only charged twenty-five dollars a lesson. His hair was long and gray and he wore sunglasses inside. He taught me the only four chords I needed to know to play "Closing Time" by Semisonic.

Closing time, this room won't be open
Till your brothers and your sisters come

As soon as I exhaust the few songs I know how to play, I start making them up as I go. *Give me a sec, I'll figure it out.*

The kids roll their eyes but stick around. Even bad music can be a real morale boost, and pretty soon, we're all in the same room—laughing, cursing, making up the world's greatest, freestyle family power-outage ballad of all time.

Hal could really play guitar which I guess is why, I never bothered picking mine up.

In times like this, I would leave the music to him—the family troubadour. But now, look at me. Look at us. Making it all fucking work in this new way. Haphazardly strumming in the darkness.

I don't have to be great to know I'm good enough. All I need is a guitar and my four chords.

———

Archer turned thirteen a month before Hal's diagnosis, when his bar mitzvah was in the early stages of planning. Knowing that the ceremony would take place while Hal was sick, we decided to have it at home. Only our closest family and friends were invited. My friends and mother took over, planned the whole thing. Chairs were delivered. Flowers and food. Succulents as centerpieces for the tables. Everything was taken care of. All I had to do was convince Hal to leave his bed and join us.

And he did. He sat down next to me and watched his son become a man in the same tallit he wore at his bar mitzvah thirty-one years earlier. When people speak of the poetry of time, this is what they mean. Like those videos of flowers blooming in slow motion beside a decaying rabbit carcass or a clip of the sun racing across the sky from its eastern entrance to its western escape. The son, stepping into his manhood just in time to hold the door open for his father to leave. Or was it Hal who was holding open the door?

Hal was weeks away from death when we passed around the challah, tore pieces off with our fingers, cinnamon sticky against our palms. *Take some and pass it on.*

In the last pictures we have as a family, we are huddled together underneath the rabbi's tallit, our friends holding it on high, their arms outstretched like sturdy trees. There was so much we didn't know. So much uncertainty, and so much to fear. Our baby becoming a man as his father became something else. But in that moment, our children crawling all over my lap, Hal's hand soft and firm in mine, we were safe.

Archer would be weeks out of his boyhood when he became the only man left in our house, the tallit folded neatly in its velvet sleeve tucked away in a drawer.

Every new beginning comes from some other beginning's end.

Archer is fifteen now. Can grow a beard if he wants. One night while shaving, he cuts himself badly, the blood dripping down his neck from his chin.

"I am here, let me help you."

"No one ever taught me to shave," he says quietly as I unfurl the toilet paper from its roll and crumple the edges of squares into tiny balls to stick against his wounds.

"Like this," I show him with the tips of my fingers.

"Don't touch them," I instruct, my voice an octave lower. "The paper will absorb the blood until it stops."

He points to the stain on the towel but I shake my head. "Don't worry, it'll come out."

Perhaps his father would know more about shaving, but all mothers know what to do with blood.

CHAPTER 15

My Bloody Valentine

In the beginning my grief felt menstrual. Thick and heavy like crimson slime.

Like a meme of the twins from *The Shining*. The flow behind them filling the hallway in slow motion, everything red.

Early on, I broke down like monthly bleeding—with different absorbencies needed for each day. Checked for stains every morning until there weren't any—another waxing and waning of the blood moon.

———

I didn't notice that my pants had period stains on them until the morning after Hal died. I bled the entire week leading up to his death. On the hospital bed as his last breath left his body. Down the hallway as I went to get the nurse. I bled in the car on the way home, toilet paper bunched up in the same underwear I had worn for a week straight, stiff with soil. Ignored the changes of clothes in my bag. Sat in my filth. Changed the toilet paper instead of my underwear. It felt like a luxury to be cracked down the middle, leaking guts.

Taking care of my body while his was deteriorating felt selfish and wrong. Like eating in front of a man who could no longer swallow. Like brushing my teeth knowing that within a matter of days, his would be burned to dust. I had the privilege of staining clothes I would eventually wash. To stink up a body I would soon shower off. Scrub with my own hands. Stand on my own legs. Under the same hot water that a week after his death would still be billed to his name.

This was the beginning of my *mourning period*, as I later described it. Four months of bleeding for, at minimum, three whole weeks every month.

I bled through my pajama pants onto the sheets. I bled throughout our entire trip to Arch Cape, my soggy interior soaking through the crotches of my yoga pants, tampon runs at gas stations, oversized sweatshirts that covered my ass, just in case.

I bled all over my hands and legs, striping the inside of my sweatpants. I bled all over Hal's favorite flannel, which I wore around my waist for an entire year after his death, rubbing the tied knot like a baby blanket, pulling on loose strings. *What's black and white and red all over.* And over and over.

I spent a large part of my marriage finding ways to be selfish in private. To do things for me that WERE ONLY MINE. I built a secret room behind the bookshelf and, when no one was looking, pulled on a leatherbound book and disappeared. Perhaps that is why the first thing I did when Hal died was knock down every wall. I set my house on fire so that the only room left was the room behind the bookshelf—the room only I knew was there.

"This is where I'm going to live from now on," I hear myself say out loud.

In my new home, I will not hide. I will not shrink myself nor prioritize people's pleasure over my own. Never again will I live in discomfort for the comfort of everyone else. Before I am even a mother, I will be *me*.

In this house, we will not become stumps in order to keep each other warm. We will remain trees.

And instead of saying these words out loud to my children, I will show them.

As a woman first, I will show them.

———

I was only a woman legally for five years before I became a wife. *Legally*. Is there such thing as an illegal woman? When I was seventeen, is that what I was?

"You legal?" men would ask in passing.

"Can't wait until she's legal."

"You know what they say, Jim. If grass is on the field, play ball."

The college boys, or anyone who was over eighteen, would call me and my friends "jailbait" while grabbing the bulges in their pants, wagging their tongues from the open windows of their cars.

"When do you turn eighteen, again?" they asked us, drunk at parties.

When I was eighteen, I had my first breast reduction surgery. I was desperate to remove the parts of myself that in the course of two years had taken over my life—replacing me, the girl, with her, the woman I wasn't ready to become. My teenage body was a paradox of power and powerlessness. The same breasts that could net free popsicles from the snack bar at the beach would have to pay for them later with looks and comments and boys who *accidentally* fell against my chest.

I was groped at parties, ogled at supermarkets. I once left a concert braless because someone on the floor of the mosh pit had pulled it off my body through my sleeve. I was supposed to be flattered by the attention. That's what they told me with my tits in their hands, *these are compliments.*

And sometimes they felt like they were. There was a sort of high to that kind of power. To knowing my body was effective in this one way. Which was what made it so confusing. It became so commonplace—the gawking and the touching and the commentary—that, during my senior year, I just waved like an idiot in my plastic tiara as a stadium full of boys on the visitor side chanted, "nice tits, queenie" during halftime at homecoming. That night something in me snapped. I stormed off the field, went home to change into my boyfriend's oversized ZERO sweatshirt and hit up the local Barnes and Noble to study. *You think you know who I am? Fuck you.*

I made it two entire years with my natural breasts before I couldn't handle them anymore. At eighteen, a plastic surgeon put me under and removed more than half of my breast tissue, taking me from an H cup to a C. What a relief it was to feel like I could wear my body in public again.

"You want to see some tits? I'll show you some tits."

When you're a girl with the body of a woman, the eyes of your beholders tell you repeatedly that you belong to everyone except yourself. This was my way of saying NO. *I belong to me. This is my body now. Mangled by choice.* Now when you look at me, you will see keloids out the sides of my bikini top. You will see scars the size of thumbs. You will know that my *face is up here.* And my tits are fucking GONE.

At the time, I told everyone I was having the surgery because I was in so much pain. "My breasts are too heavy for my back," I explained. But that wasn't true. As soon as I was able to *capitalize on* the surge of power my "developed" body allotted me, I was also able to recognize that it wasn't my power at all.

It was the first of many paralyzing realizations that to be a woman in the world, I had to be willing to sacrifice parts of my body. Drains-of-blood-and-guts-hanging-off-the-sides-of-my-chest-bandages—willing. Unable-to-breastfeed-all-four-of-my-children—willing. Bras-during-sex-so-I-didn't-have-to-explain-my-scars—willing.

Now, that *will* is a war. I have been hit and am wandering around the battlefield looking for something to stop the bleeding. Looking for someone to insert themselves into the part of my body I am expected to close off.

There's an old friend I was always attracted to. I think maybe it's mutual because, whenever our paths cross, we end up stuck together, the crowd shape shifting around us as we push against the limits of flirtation. He has never even slightly crossed the line with me and is the kind of gentleman who wouldn't dare. Even though he knew Hal and I had a tumultuous marriage. Even though I confided in him on multiple occasions that I wanted to leave. Even though Hal stood back and glared at us, assuming, and rightfully so, that I was not to be trusted.

I didn't expect to see him at Hal's funeral but there he suddenly was. He had lost both his parents to cancer, one after the other, and knew more than most what my last four months had looked like. He understood me in a way most people didn't. He also knew about my marriage. And when he looked at me across the grieving crowd, I felt seen.

I would have fucked him in the bathroom, if I could. I would have hiked up my black dress in the alley of the Whiskey and bled all over his hands. Instead we hugged each other in the foyer of the venue and it took me much longer than was appropriate to let go.

It didn't take long for our texts to become overtly sexual. I, of course, was the one who initiated. I didn't even try to play it cool. I was on fire. I wanted him. I always did.

Come here and take me against the side of my house.

And, yes, I know it's very late.

And raining.

But I cannot leave my children and my side yard is fully sheltered.

Bring a coat. We'll figure it out.

For several weeks, I texted him when the kids were asleep and he drove over and knocked on the gate as I waited outside, parka down to my knees with nothing underneath, my breath like smoke against the darkness as he pushed toward me, blowing on his hands to warm them before sliding them up my legs and under my coat.

The first time he touched me, I had to brace myself to keep from falling down. It had been years since someone touched me like that—since I had wanted to be touched—possessed by a deep yearning to be eviscerated by someone else's body. He could have eaten me alive and I would have thanked him.

But it was more than just an arousal—it was an awakening. It was a wallop of relief that I was on the other side of all the yesterdays. To feel, for the first time in my life, the independence of being in my own motherfucking body.

I was FREE. In my own house. In my own life. On my own terms. The carnal energy shift felt like its own kind of death. A black hole had formed, and with the insertion of two fingers, everything that had come before was sucked down deep into the void, ground up, and spat out in moans. The rain was coming down harder and it didn't matter that we were outside against the wall of my dark house.

I was the eye of the storm, opening.

And from every slit in my body, tears fell and carried me away.

I bleed on every man I fuck for the next several months. In the past, this would have made me feel embarrassed, unclean, self-conscious. Now it feels exactly right.

My body is doing what it's supposed to do. I am shedding my insides like a snake who has turned herself inside out. My truth looks like rust on the thick of my thighs.

"Your bloody valentine."

Nobody seems to mind. Occasionally someone will stop. "You're bleeding," they'll say, and I'll say yes, you're right. This is true. Welcome to my body. She is under construction. Pardon her appearance.

Showing up in defiant opposition to all feelings once repressed, I leave heart-shaped stains on the beds of men I will never see again. I have gone from noun to verb.

My ob-gyn doesn't know that Hal has died. I can tell because he greets me in my paper gown as if nothing has happened.

"Rebecca! How have you been?"

Occasionally, I run into people who don't know and I have to tell them about the death and it never gets easier even though I feel like it should.

"Something terrible has happened," I say, choking back tears.

Dr. Wright delivered all three of my daughters. He placed our girls gently into Hal's hands before I was even able to touch them. I think about that a lot—how the first hands they touched were not mine. I think about Hal's words when Fable was born—how beautiful he told me she was. I think of him with our twins. The cracks in his voice, the emotion.

"You did it, hon," he said.

My doctor gives me a Kleenex to wipe my eyes. I tell him I have been bleeding pretty much on and off since the night in the hospital when Hal died.

"Four months."

Apparently, this is normal, but he tells me my copper IUD is making it worse.

"I think we should take it out," he tells me.

We make plans to replace it with an IUD with hormones. He offers to pull my copper one that day, but I'd rather bleed profusely than risk pregnancy, so I decline.

"You can pull it next month when the new IUD is back in stock."

I ask for an STD test. It's been many years since I've taken one and everything is different now. Today, people list their STIs in dating apps. A potential date will ask for your test results if the conversation is simply *going well*. I am blown away by the transparency. I don't remember it being like that before I got married. I am in awe.

———

A month later, I get a call from the doctor's office letting me know my IUD just came in and is ready for insertion. I wait in a room surrounded by pregnant women cradling the roundness of new worlds, some flanked by partners nervously shifting against orange pleather.

I fold my arms over my own waistline and nod in solidarity. I am preparing for a kind of birth too.

The nurse calls my name and I follow her into the room with the ultrasound machine. I strip down to my paper robe, dig my heels into the metal stirrups, and wait for my doctor to remove one IUD and replace it with another. The changing of the guard.

Over the course of several weeks, my periods become unnaturally light before disappearing almost completely. The gleam of a single pink splotch when I wipe.

It reminds me of how I bled after all three pregnancies, my body clearing itself of the remnants of what it takes to grow a life. How everything that was inside of me was suddenly gone. That after the swelling and puking, the pushing and tearing, all that remained was a smear of afterbirth between my legs, which I dabbed at gently until I healed.

CHAPTER 16

First Dates

Everything I was ever told about sex and love was wrong, but my mother certainly did her best. She answered every question with transparency and a matter-of-fact shamelessness that embarrassed me but never made me feel like I was anything other than a normal teenage girl. If I came to her with blood stains on my sheets, she shrugged and wrapped them up in her arms—nothing to see here, wink wink, move right along. She never once questioned the padded bras I pulled off the sale racks at Target and threw in the cart nor did she shame my need to apply MAC's Spanish Fly lipstick from the front seat of her minivan on my first day of seventh grade. When I insisted on redecorating my room with sexually explicit perfume ads torn from the pages of *Cosmo* and *Seventeen*, she complimented my design aesthetic.

She, like all mothers of girls, was given a choice: she could either stifle or support her daughter. To be her defendant or prosecutor under the laws of patriarchy, a system so ingrained that it was impossible not to stumble upon one of its trip wires.

My mother understood that girls became women. That being her daughter was only part of my story, just like being my mother was only part of hers. And while I never doubted her support for me or felt shamed in any way by anything that came out of her mouth, her sex talks—which fit within her own parameters of life experience—weren't exactly empowering.

"You will be ready to have sex when you are in a loving, committed relationship," she told me, hoping I would wait until I was, at the very least, in love.

But love for me came easy. I fell in love with everyone. In eighth grade, I devoted an entire journal to a boy named Shane who played guitar every Friday night at Java Depot, his long blonde hair cascading down his back as he whisper-sang Smashing Pumpkins covers. A boy who didn't even know me by name. A boy I would have run away with had he asked. Just like that, me sitting shotgun in his white Toyota pickup truck. *Take me. I'm yours, Java Shane.*

Even at fourteen years old, justifying readiness for sex with "falling in love" didn't seem right. Love destroyed whatever independence I had, turning me into an attention monster. I was a girl so fixated on her boyfriend's health and happiness, it took me months to notice I was sabotaging my own. It is so easy to take from girls who know how to love. Candy from babies. Be mine, Valentine. So began the struggle of finding love, feeling trapped, planning my escape, running away, and starting over.

———

Four months after Hal dies, I sign up for Tinder. My profile is blunt and effective. "I am newly widowed and DTF. *Possibly with you.*" I make it clear I am only here for one thing, which is societally unacceptable for a woman in my position, but I don't want anyone to get it twisted. And being clear from the get-go on a dating app seems like a good place to start.

My name is Rebecca and I'm a thirty-seven-year-old Gemini in Los Angeles and, *yeah, I am that kind of girl.*

The last time I did any kind of online dating was in the early days of nerve.com, when it felt more like experimenting with a new drug than legitimately connecting with a potential partner. In those days, we dialed up to connect to our Hotmail accounts, filtering our photos the old-fashioned way, with creative lighting and facial piercings.

A few months into internet dating, which was more like one-night standing, I did fall for someone I met. He was a writer who wore a rattail down his back, worshipped David Foster Wallace, and regularly quizzed my literary knowledge of dead white men. A cliché of red flags. He was charming and clever, condescending and arrogant, exactly my type at the time, which might explain how I so easily convinced myself that his tendency toward sarcastic misogyny was something different than *actual* misogyny.

One night, after fucking me on his kitchen floor, he told me he had been dating someone else, that they were now in love, and this was the last time *we should do this.* His dick was still hard inside me.

"Okay, that's fine," I said maintaining my cool-girl chill, body clenched to keep from breaking down in front of him.

I gathered my clothes as he watched me in silence, the smoke from his joint curling around the blades of the ceiling fan, its light bulbs matted with dust.

Years later, when I experienced some early success monetizing my personal blog, he reached out to me out of nowhere asking for help. I didn't answer. After several days, he followed up in all caps. "NO RESPONSE, HUH? OH, I SEE HOW IT IS, BITCH."

If only, I typed back and saved to drafts.

IF. ONLYYYYYYYYYY.

That was the end of my internet-dating tenure. It was 2002 and I was twenty-one-years old taking dating cues from season five of *Sex and the City*.

I couldn't help but wonder, if love was something that happened in real life, was the internet just an emotionally stunted counterfeit purse? Surely, the Christian Dior saddlebag of my dreams was out there somewhere. Or at the very least, a trim little monogrammed Fendi baguette.

———

Sixteen years later and *hey guys, I'm back*. This time as an adult woman who, hopefully, knows better.

One of the first people I match with is a Mike, a widower who is passionate about architecture and artisanal coffee. I am not particularly attracted to him, but he is the first and only widower I have seen on a dating app and I think, at the very least, maybe we can be friends. I don't know a single person even roughly my age who has lost a spouse or a partner, so I feel like we'll have a lot to talk about—an ideal entry person into the dating space. I'm elated. He is, too. Our messages back and forth are in all caps.

We agree to meet for coffee. I purposefully set our meeting an hour before I have to leave to pick up my kids from school. This way, I have a real out and, if the date goes well, I won't be tempted to spend the rest of the day with a stranger. It doesn't even occur to me that the date could be a bust. I assume that our crossing paths this early in my journey is a sign. What are the chances that a handful of swipes into my first dating app, I would find someone with such a similar story?

But the moment I walk into the cafe, I know this is wrong.

He is nothing like his pictures and I recoil at the thought of being seen with him in public—a thirty-something man in cuffed wide-leg blue jeans.

Then I do what I always do, berate myself for being shallow—for not giving this stranger a chance.

What if he's extremely kind? Let's give this Sketchers-clad widower a go!

So instead of leaving when I think I should, I say yes to a latte and join him on the patio.

Before we are even seated, his phone is in my hand. He wants to show me a picture and I squint trying to make out the screen.

It's a selfie he took—his face heavily bearded and smiling like a tourist at Disney World as he stood over the corpse of his newly deceased wife.

———

When I was twenty years old, I lived in a studio apartment in Hollywood. My building had no parking, which meant I routinely parked my car several blocks away, usually at night, when street parking was hard to come by. I would speed walk home, all my senses on heightened alert, keys held between fingers—the trick every girl is taught to do. But in the light of day, I felt safe. I could see what was coming. People are different in the afternoon.

One day, in the unsuspecting light, a Cadillac pulled out, cornering me just as I was crossing Bronson south of Hollywood Boulevard.

"Hey, there. You think you can help me with something? I need to find my way back to my hotel. I'm lost."

Those were the days when men pulled over and asked for directions. When all they had were paper maps and unsuspecting girls on the sides of roads to assist them.

"Sure. Where do you need to go?"

I approached his car willingly, a bright-eyed compass delighted to help a man with no sense of direction, but within a couple feet of his car, I realized which one of us was lost.

He had shifted his body to the side so he was kneeling on the driver's seat with his purpled penis in his hand.

"Look at it," he said. "LOOK AT IT."

I said nothing, turned around, and walked casually in the opposite direction of my house. Like *whatever, man, your dick doesn't scare me.* Took a turn into an alley so he wouldn't know where I lived and entered through the back of the building where he couldn't see me. I didn't make a sound the rest of the day. Stayed silent into the night. Just brushed my teeth. Got into bed. Closed my eyes.

I am paralyzed in the same way with Mike and his dead wife's photos. Like he's showing me something he knows he shouldn't. Trying to shock me by exposing himself. *Showing me* is his kink. I say nothing as he scrolls through his phone to show me another.

"She wasn't dead here, but, you know, close."

He tells me he loved her but felt that her dying was easier than the end to his prior relationship—a divorce. And I relate to that part in a way that makes me fall even more silent. He is angry and I am angry, too. He is sad and I am sad, too. And I don't know whether to run or to slowly turn my head and walk away. The truth is, I relate to more of it than I am comfortable admitting. The banality of a corpse to a caretaker. Perhaps he is just trying to relate to me. To bond. To share these photos with someone, finally, who understands.

Why was I judging him so harshly? And wasn't it true someone could just as easily do the same to me? After all, the kids and I had literally danced on Hal's grave. I was dating months after his death. I hated him. Loved him, yes, but also hated him. Went back and forth between missing him and feeling overwhelming relief to never have to deal with him again. Was I a monster? Is that the way people would perceive me once I was comfortable enough to be publicly truthful?

I cut the date short. Thank him for the coffee.

A mile down Wilshire, recognizing the hard rock of breathlessness in my chest, I pull into a strip mall off Western and have a panic attack in the parking lot. It lasts the length of two and-a-half songs and reminds me of all the things I do not know. What if the life I thought I wanted isn't the life I really want?

I miss Hal. I want to tell him how batshit fucking crazy this dude was. We would have had so much fun laughing about this—about all of this. *Please come back. Can you hear me? Give me a sign that you're still here. Play me something you loved on the radio.*

But he doesn't. It's just me and the music I always listened to alone. He didn't even know any of these songs.

CHAPTER 17

The Tenderness of One-Night Stands

After Mike, I go about things differently. I do not rush into meeting anyone in person, even those with whom I feel compatible. I give us all room to breathe. To impress each other or become estranged through a series of unreturned text messages.

Josh is the second person I agree to meet—this time for a drink. He is in an open relationship which will become somewhat of a pre-requisite when it comes to who I feel comfortable dating. I am only interested in casual connections with those seeking same.

Josh is a single divorced dad who raised his children almost entirely on his own. They are all grown up now, but I feel like he understands more than most where I'm coming from. We make plans to meet in a dim bar on his side of town. I'm running late, as usual, and he tells me no rush when I text him from my Lyft. It will never not be awkward meeting someone in person for the first time but I immediately relax upon spotting him in the corner booth, relieved that he looks like the same man in his pictures.

Josh is shy, sexy, with sculptor's hands, rough like conch shells. Protruding knuckles, fingers flat against black jeans. He's old enough to be my father but there is something specifically boyish about him. Or maybe he's just lived in Silverlake so long he's mastered the art of aging backwards. Another messy-haired artisan Peter Pan in horn-rimmed glasses. Josh reminds me of the men I chased in my youth when I lied about my age. When waking up in the arms of middle-aged men made me feel like a *real woman*. When getting dressed in the blue light of dawn against a puckered, leather couch felt like the height of maturity, like playing dress up with the skins of my future selves. Waking up to the smell of someone else's coffee made me feel like the kinda girl a man might want to take care of, even though it was always the other way around. These were the kinds of paradoxes I mulled over during every harshly lit walk of shame.

Josh and I speak freely and effortlessly, our familial stories similarly complicated. We both married young. He has twins, too. He is modest about his recent success. The studio downtown. We make tentative plans we both know we won't keep about me checking out his space. We sip our drinks and brush our hands against each other accidentally on purpose until finally, buzzing with tension, we lock eyes and he asks if I *wanna get outta here.*

I respond by standing up, while he tips back what's left of his drink. We spend the rest of the evening at his place, in the loft he built himself. He rolls us a joint, bare-assed on gray sheets, and we fuck on and off for hours against the stains of my blood, his body thrashing around like a caught fish. When it's over I reach for him, light nails against his back while he catches his breath, twitches, smiles, his skin temporarily stained pink from the guts I don't apologize for.

"The blood will come out," I whisper.

"I know," he says, lighting the cigarette he shares with me in a bed I'll never see again.

We have been told—conditioned, really—to believe that these kinds of encounters are empty. Hollow. That they detach us from our humanity—keep us cold. We validate relationships based on commitment—of time and money and dinner reservations. On taking it slow. A good woman takes it slow.

But I feel nothing but tenderness for this man I barely know—for this momentary exchange. The sharing of smoke. It is extremely possible to fully connect with an experience that is momentary and short lived. I would even argue that, for some of us, such interludes are even more profound. To begin and then end in one night: yes.

We catch our breath and exchange words, trace our fingers over each other's moistened bodies. Bodies we will inevitably forget. Dry off with the same sheet, adjust wild hair, negotiate our departure. There is an equity that sticks in the low light of afterward. Even the most threatening man becomes almost infantile after sex. He becomes gentle, regardless of what it took to get him there. If he assumed power before this moment, it's now gone. *Where did it go? Do I get to keep it? Is it mine now?*

Maybe this is why I've always liked this part. The after. The kiss goodbye. The going home.

When I leave, we hug goodbye. Make plans neither of us will keep. Say thank you. That was fun.

Josh generously offers to call me an Uber home and I accept. We will never see or speak to each other again.

———

Later that night, when I come home sometime after 2 a.m., my son is waiting up for me, ankles crossed, video-game controller in hand.

"Shit, you scared me."

"You're home late."

"Didn't the babysitter tell you to go to bed?"

"No, Mom," he says, "I'm thirteen now."

"Oh. Okay."

And I keep my distance so that he can't smell the man on me. I tell him I love him from the safety of the hallway, hustle into the bathroom, turn on the shower, lock the door. What is the name for this, I think, washing the sex out of my hair? It's primal, this feeling. I'm an animal who must wash a stranger's scent from her body. Even in the shower, I am on heightened alert until I am sure the man has been fully scrubbed off my skin. Until I have conquered every inch of my body with soap. Fingerprints down the drain, leave no trace.

This soon becomes a pattern. I go out. Archer waits up. I hustle toward the bathroom before he appears in the hallway.

"Be right out!" I say, stripping down to nothing, bra slung over the porcelain of the bathtub.

"I love you. I'll be right there."

I spoke very candidly about dating with my kids from the beginning. I wanted them to know the truth. Maybe not every detail—my privacy was also important—but I wanted them to know that I was living my life. That now that I was their sole caretaker, I needed to spend some time every week taking care of myself.

Four months had passed since Hal died, but it had been years since I'd been intimate with anyone. I was finding my way back to myself, I explained to them.

"What are you wearing? Is this new?"

"No. I've always had this. I've just never put it on before."

Now that their dad isn't here, I want to try all of my outfits.

They had questions, of course.

"Was I looking for a new husband?"

"No. Never. I don't want to ever marry again."

I told them about the years I wanted a divorce. How every time their dad and I fought, I would plan my escape. That I should have left years ago but didn't. That marriages are complicated and not for everyone.

I talked to my children like human beings because that is what they are. And while I was always particularly good at being overtly truthful with my children, Hal's death further pushed me into the "tell the whole truth, especially when your voice quakes" camp.

I never wanted them to feel anything but included—to feel safe to come to me with secrets, which is why I told them mine. I told them I cheated on their dad. That even though I was sad, I felt free.

This was the hardest part for people to understand. How could you possibly do such a thing? Your kids know that you're dating? That you're having sex? That you're a human woman outside of being their mother?

And the answer was mostly yes. Certainly, I talked to all four of my children differently—age appropriately and almost always in conversations they solicited.

I believed that it was important for them to know the truth—and I was prepared to be judged for it.

I am not ashamed to have been human in my marriage and to remain human on the other side of it. I love you. But you also need to know that I am so many different kinds of things. I am so many different women. I am not just a parent and when you grow up—if you choose to have kids of your own—you won't be, either.

Katie is the kind of woman who wears suits to weddings. Seamlessly fusing femme and butch, her profile on Bumble is a collection of snappy one-liners and profile pics that feature a crooked little smile smirking out from under knit hats. Swoon.

When we match, I immediately launch into my life story. Explain to her that I was married to a man for years and, while I do have some experience with women, it's limited and has only ever occurred under the gaze of men. She comments on my SOMETHING CASUAL status and I admit to her that, yes, I'm sort of *just here for one thing.*

It is the first time I have admitted this to a woman I might potentially date and I immediately recoil at the thought of objectifying her. It is one thing to make these kinds of sweeping generalizations to men, who I have always had complicated relationships with, and quite another to confess what I'm after to a woman, who by default of her gender, I respect in a way that may or may not sound contradictory to my intentions. So I backtrack. Explain to her that it isn't personal. And I totally understand if...

But she's not precious about it and tells me not to be either, picking up where I left off with my story to generously share hers back. She tells me, just as honestly, that she is also only here for one thing.

And that thing is a relationship.

We still agree to meet for a date—albeit a daytime one. At the very least, we can become friends—something, I realize, I have never discussed with a man. Is it because I do not desire friendship with men? Is it because, when I got married, I abandoned my male friendships for Hal's and no longer know how to make friends with men on my own? Have I lost the will to connect to men platonically? And, if so, what am I modeling for my children? I want to surround them with good men who are lovely and kind, but I also have this animalian instinct to keep all men away from us in case they prove me wrong. So often, they have proved me wrong.

I wasn't always this way. I used to feel I could relate wholly to men, but my marriage shifted something in me and now I don't remember how.

Sex is one thing. But intimacy, connection, safety, and long-term companionship now feels more attainable with women. Perhaps I am not as straight as my sexual history suggests. Is this why women make me feel nervous? Like sitting down with someone who understands so much of my experience—who doesn't need to ask questions to know where I've been.

Katie is tiny in person. With boots on, I'm a good foot taller than she is, which I'm . . . into? We hug each other. Take our seats. Make small talk. She's late and so am I (always) but she has a much better reason.

"I made you a present."

"You what?"

Katie sticks her hand into a giant canvas bag and pulls out an 8 x 10 paper certificate, complete with gold seal stamp. My name is printed in large Olde English font. Below it, the words: *Congratulations on your first real date with a woman.*

"I know we're just meeting here as friends," she tells me, "but it still counts."

I'm so moved by the gesture, I begin to weep. This woman. (A stranger!) Meets me for coffee. Knowing that this will go nowhere. And yet, she still makes me a gift. Not just a gift—a proclamation. A certificate that says I SEE YOU. WELCOME TO YOUR NEW LIFE. Just because. JUST BECAUSE!

"This is beyond! I can't believe you did this!"

"Come on," she says, "I had to commemorate the occasion!"

"Well, thank you. This is definitely going on the fridge."

Soon after Katie, I will meet a polyamorous woman who is looking for my same kind of casual. We will date sporadically for several months. Meet in the back row of movie theatres. Wear skirts.

One afternoon, after it's been there for several weeks, Fable asks me about the certificate on the refrigerator.

"You a lesbian now?"

"Not a lesbian. Just . . . open to everyone."

"Oh," she says, "So you're pan."

"Sure."

"No, not sure. That's what you are. You can say it out loud to me. Look at me, I'm listening."

"Yes, okay. You're right. That's what I am."

"Good for you," Fable smiles. "And Mama?"

"Yeah?"

Fable hands me a jar.

"Can you open this?"

Despite my flippancy for naming my sexuality, I do not take this lightly. So many human beings have had to fight and die in order to say such seemingly innocuous things aloud. I know my lightness has a history of heaviness. The stories of queer ancestors leading secret lives have been whispered between women my entire life. The mother's mothers. Diaries locked and then burned. I carry their stories.

———

In the months after Hal died, I meet two different men who have been victims of abuse. Ben tells me the first time we meet. With Matt, I find out on my own, when after our date, we go back to his place and he lies down on his bed, closes his eyes, and tells me *to do whatever I want to do to his body.*

At first, I am stunned. Don't know whether to leave or to stay. I have never been in a situation quite like this and I am immediately turned off but, also, I feel like I should help him. He looks like he might cry.

His body is vulnerable. Dick still soft. I harden him, fumble in his top drawer for a condom, and climb on top of his body, riding him slowly. I do not ask him to open his eyes. Instead, I fuck him until he comes, knowing I will not. That I cannot in this position. That this is for me, too, but in a different kind of way. He is not a small man but here, beneath my body, I could crush him.

It's okay, I whisper. And he nods.

I am torn between feeling like I should and shouldn't have done this. He seems to need it more than I do but when I leave him, I later feel like I have done something against my own will to satiate his.

Where does one draw the line with a mercy fuck? Did I help him or hurt him? And what about my feelings? Why did I shelve them the moment I took one look at his apartment and felt needed in a very different way? And would he—a man facing the same situation—do the same thing?

I think of all the times I faked orgasms to make men feel like they knew how to fuck me. All the times I said yes but meant no. The times I slept with men I felt sorry for, lending my body out like it was never mine to begin with. Like the way my grandmothers lent out their handkerchiefs when somebody sneezed in a room with no tissues.

Here. Take this. Just give it back to me when you're done.

———

Ben is different. We meet in person for the first time in the light of day. My profile was refreshing, he tells me, *honest*, so in turn, he will be the same with me.

I realize as he proceeds to tell me his story that men do not talk about sexual abuse the way women do. I am stunned to receive him like this. He is younger than I am by nearly a decade, but his grace ages him. His willingness to trust me. I realize I have had the same "yes, I've been assaulted" conversation with almost every woman I know, but this is the first time I've had it with a man.

"Sex is . . . hard for me, sometimes. There are certain things I cannot do because of triggers. I'm still working through it all . . ."

I listen to him. And while I can relate to parts of his story, I am struck by how different it is for a man to have to carry an experience like that without the solidarity or understanding of his peers.

"I will not pretend to know what it feels like to have had your experience and I'm sorry."

Men are called brave for so much less.

Later that week we go out for our second date. And after drinks I walk back with him to his place, where I ask him if he's comfortable with me making the first move.

"Does this feel okay? Are you sure? How about this . . . ?"

I want to do everything right by him, but I can't help but ask questions. I am a mother, after all. And while I am not supposed to fuck like one, I guess I sort of do.

"You can tell me to stop, okay? If it starts to feel bad to you."

But it doesn't. He just looks at me and I look at him. *I can be safe for you*, I tell him with my hands. *This can feel okay.*

I think of all the times men should have asked the same of me. It is so blatantly obvious to me that this person requires a different kind of touch. This is not the kind of man you ask to choke you, for example. This is the kind of man you drag your body over. Like a blanket. This is the kind of man you hold with both arms while whispering his name.

Do you like this? How about this?

You are safe here. I promise. You are safe.

Months later, he meets someone and falls in love. He texts me excitedly about it, and I send him an animated GIF of a woman with bangs clapping her hands.

Daniel and I go on three dates. On the first one, we meet halfway between our homes. We have a couple drinks before "going for a walk" and ending up in the backseat of his car. I feel like I'm in high school. We go to second base. Or maybe it's third. I always get my bases mixed up. I like him enough to want to see him again. He seems to feel the same. The second date, we meet for dinner. We go to a movie at an art-house theater and are two of only a dozen people in attendance. Afterward, we sit in the backseat and make out even more. I put his hand between my legs. He is tall and wild-haired, tattooed, and band-shirted. If I had a type this would be the one. Which makes him more of a liability than the rest of them. He's someone I might actually fall for and, for a moment, I get carried away.

On our third date, I go to his house. I wear a shirt that buttons up in the back that he can't figure out how to take off. It's sweet. We laugh. He makes my drink himself with mint from his garden. He has a perfect dick. We get high and fuck in his bed. His floors are spotless, and his records appear to be arranged in alphabetical order. I think of what my house would look like to him. Broken crayons and books shoved into shelves at all directions. *LOL*, I think. *I will never bring this one home.*

There is a certain relief that comes with recognizing that a person is all wrong in one way but right in another. Daniel doesn't know where I live. He doesn't know what my life looks like or any of my friends. He knows that I have children. I wait for commentary on my caesarian scar—from him and everyone else—the faint line above the racing stripe of pubic hair. Slightly crooked faded reminder of all the things he can't see. *Once upon a time, it opened like a mouth.*

In the beginning, I wanted to hide the proof that I was, indeed, a mother. But in time, I took the fingers of strangers and traced the line for them. *If you want to look at me, look at this, too.* So that they might know that I can exist in two different kinds of skin at once. That I am my own kind of woman regardless of how many children I once wore inside my flesh. That carrying life and expelling it into the world isn't the only reason my body is a body. That there's an entire organ whose sole purpose is pleasure. *Here, give me your fingers so that I can trace them against that, too.*

In the thirty-minute drive home from his house to mine, I get to talking to the woman driving my Lyft. I am always relieved when I find out my driver is a woman. For myself, sure, but also for her. I think about all the drunk men she might have picked up instead. It's after 2 a.m. on a Friday night, after all. Rush hour for the last-call boys.

Her name is Mary and she wants to know where I was and what I was doing. I hesitate for a moment before I dive all fuck-it-style into my complicated life and current adventures.

I tell her that my husband has only been dead a handful of months, but this is what I've wanted for so long and I'm just, you know, living. And having these amazing encounters with strangers and, yes, it's possible to connect with people in that way. And, *no, I don't think I'll ever see them again. What would be the point? We got to be perfect for each other for a few hours and there is something holy about that.*

Casual sex can be like . . . the ultimate living-in-the-moment experience. No need for past histories. Or future expectations. Just two people falling on top of each other until they decide to stand up.

Mary explains to me that she is married to a man she wants to leave. She has taken a second job driving at night because he refuses to work. She sleeps three hours at most, she tells me, and then she bursts into tears.

I ask her if she wants to pull the car over so we can talk. I climb into the front seat and, beneath the glow of the 76 gas station sign, I explain to her that I wanted the same thing for years and that I, too, was afraid I couldn't make it on my own. And then we come up with a plan for her to leave him.

Weeks later, Daniel will meet and fall in love with someone else. A year later they will get engaged on Christmas morning. Glossy like a postcard. Perfectly matched.

But this moment, right here in this car, is why my experience with Daniel feels so profound. I have always connected deeply with people through the charge I get from casual encounters. Something about the exchange of energy—I feel most alive on the other side of such experiences. The adrenaline of freedom is contagious and all I want to do is pass it on.

Yeah, sex is cool, but have you ever conspired with your Lyft driver to plot an escape from her soul-sucking marriage at 2 a.m. on the side of Olympic Blvd.?

It was Daniel who brought me to her car and us to each other. Because of one connection, there were two. There are so many different ways to merge.

There were others like Daniel. Like Katie. Like all of them. There was sex and there was not sex. There was making out in bar bathrooms and hand jobs in the back of Lyfts. There was good sex and okay sex and dick pics and tasteful nudes cropped for anonymity. There was phone sex and sext sex ranging from incredible to mediocre to mortifyingly bad. There were men and there were women, single and married, but open, always open. And I felt something with all of them. A series of connective glimpses. The disappearance of self-consciousness in my nakedness. A tangle of shadows against the dimly lit walls. The drag of a wrist when getting up to go to the bathroom. Like second hands making up for found time, we get to be bodies here. Smashing against each other for a limited time only.

This is what home feels like for me. Like revisiting a foreign country where you can now speak the language, I am back where I started, but this time I know how to communicate my needs. How to prioritize my pleasure. How to walk away from the kind of men who will never deserve my love and also the ones who do.

It takes a certain kind of understanding and acknowledgment to welcome interactions, sexual or otherwise, knowing they will likely go nowhere—that they will live within the walls of momentary bliss. Maybe because every time we do this, we better learn to let go. We say it's okay to die. It's okay to lose. It's okay to exist in one moment and then move forward into another one. An absorption of pulse. The crash like a heartbeat. Ephemeral love is also love.

It's okay to attach yourself to me and then let go.

"Really, I want you to. Go on. *Ghost me*."

There are no more walks of shame.

CHAPTER 18

Something Casual

I didn't intend to get into anything serious. I was positively *certain* I wouldn't. Doubled down on the conviction I was incapable of loving any man, maybe ever. That I, would pursue a life where men occasionally guest starred. Maybe a cohost here and there. A brief cameo. Two weeks max.

It was settled. I had discussed the pros and cons of serious relationships at length with my heart. And even though my experiences in the aftermath of Hal's death had been mostly with gentle, respectful men. I could feel my disdain bubbling just under the surface. It wouldn't take much water in the pot to make it boil.

Instead, I would have lovers. *Lovers!* There would be lovers of all shapes, sizes, and genders who say things like "goodbye forever . . . we'll always have Paris," as I wave my hanky from the window of an outbound train. We make passionate love in all kinds of locations, mere blips on each other's timelines. Ships in the night. *I didn't even get her last name.*

"I'm the kind of girl you sleep with but don't wake up next to," I said on multiple occasions, and I believed it to be unequivocally true. Perhaps this is why I leaned on a sort of brashness in my early text exchanges with potentials. I was looking for someone who wasn't looking for someone. Someone who didn't *need* me and never would. A very specific kind of rebound.

And yet, underneath all that sardonic hutzpah and stubborn pride was a person with a soft-boiled interior who yearned to be loved, albeit differently than before. Anyone who heard me so adamant in my claims of emotionless connection would have rolled their eyes, seeing me for exactly who I was—a broken woman whose "never evers" would amount to "I told you sos."

The lady doth protest too much.

I could hide the keys, but eventually my bleeding heart would find a way to sneak past the security guard and escape through the slats of my bones. I was always capable of being loved and loving back. My version just looked different than the one I was told I should want.

It was why *free will* was so important to me. I knew in my depths how vulnerable I was—how easy I fell in (and out) of love with people and how out of control I felt when I did. I knew I was capable of hurting others. Of lying and cheating and becoming disinterested in putting in the kind of work long-term relationships need to thrive.

———

It is hard to know what kind of love is possible when all you've ever known is something else. The kind of love I wanted and needed was a kind of love I had yet to experience and didn't know existed.

And it was the kind of love I found with Jake.

The night we met, there was a windstorm so severe that the outdoor furniture picked up and smashed against the windows next to where we were sitting. The glass didn't break but, there we were, up and out of our seats as the furniture rattled the restaurant.

The wind was so strong I had to cover my face when we walked back to his car. *Can you believe this weather?* Nothing felt real. I didn't know how I felt about him, but I knew there was something—that this wasn't like the other dates, the other nights. This was the kind of man you let take you home. This was a beginning.

Jake was my first ever southern gentleman. He was soft-spoken and mild mannered, with a slight drawl that sounded like butter. He had the kind of calm dad humor that would have incited multiple eye rolls at dinner if it wasn't so elegantly delivered—Jake, I assumed, was the kind of gentleman caller who wouldn't make the first move. And, when he did, his first of many surprises, it proved how little I knew of his caliber of men.

Our first kiss reminded me of being thirteen years old—when kissing was enough—when mouths pressed together equaled love equaled *I'll never wash these lips again* equaled me under my Laura Ashley sheets feeling invincible. Young heart flexing in front of my giant mirrors, *look at me. I found everything I've ever wanted and more.* It was the kind of kiss that exhausted me. Suddenly I felt like I needed to lie down. So, I did. Face down in his lap.

He was the first man I met that I wanted to come inside. Into my house. Into my life. Into my body.

Nothing was the same after that. He didn't live in LA yet. He was just here for the month between jobs. We spent as much time together as we could while he was here, and then he was gone.

I told him from the beginning that, if we were to do this, I wanted to keep it open. Nonmonogamous. That I wanted to continue to date and hoped he would, too. We were on the same page. And then we were on the same page again. And again and again until I lost track of all the things we believed in that were the same—an entire book of things. Most importantly, a mutual love language: freedom.

We spent our time apart making each other mixtapes, adding and then removing all the love songs so as not to scare the other off. It was instantly understood that we didn't belong to each other. That our hearts and our bodies were our own.

———

On our first date, Jake wanted to know what Hal called me so he could call me something different. "Bec. He called me Bec."

It caught me off guard at first, this ask. But then I understood. He wanted to show me that he wasn't trying to replace my husband who had only been dead a handful of months. He didn't want to trigger any feelings in me, to apply pressure to the parts of me that were raw.

"How about Be," he asked. "Has anyone ever called you Be?"

"No, but I like it. Thank you."

———

When you have spent the bulk of your adult life in a tumultuous marriage it is very hard to understand its toxicity, until its over and you're out the other side. For me, falling in love with a man who was not only kind but *communicative*, caring, and concerned about my feelings was such a shock to my system that I became both euphoric and furious. I was no longer with a man who knew exactly what to say to tear me down but, instead, went out of his way to lift me up and *listen*.

My relief and gratitude were transcendent. But within that was the trigger for a new kind of grief—one that was rooted in self-hatred and just as paralyzing. I had gone most of my life trying to be the right kind of woman for the wrong kind of man. And as relieved as I was to have found the opposite in a new life I got to build from scratch, I was also ashamed that I had spent so many of my years normalizing abuse.

I apologized to myself. To my children. I was terrified that I had modeled acquiescence to my daughters and rage to my son. I was relieved to have a man around them who wasn't like their father. But saying those words out loud was too painful, so instead I said things like, "this is the only kind of man I will allow into our home from now on."

I didn't believe that men like Jake existed. That someone would want to explore the kind of open, nonmonogamous relationship I knew I needed. And I certainly didn't think it would happen this fast—six months into my post-wife life.

Compersion is when you feel joyful for a person you love when they are feeling joy and love with someone else. It goes against everything we're taught about "cheaters" and "jealousy," but to me, it is beautiful. Generous. Sacred. It contradicts every patriarchal, traditionally pushed ideal. Perhaps this is why it felt so equitable. Loving. We were making up rules up as we went. We were also breaking them, changing them, learning how to live without them within social circles that upheld them mightily. Together.

With Jake, honesty was met with reward as opposed to shame. And during a time when I felt so alone with my strange, indecipherable grief, this was a revelation. I was a free woman who was also in love with a man. I felt brand new. A woman thriving in the open air of second chances where the rules of others did not apply.

Sex and love had found a way to cohabitate in this new realm. I could experience deep love for someone without limitation. And, by some miracle, he felt the same. We would each go out with other people and come back to each other, our bodies learning to do things they never knew were possible. Communicating about every pleasure and pain, every want and need.

Jake and I made plans to have dates with other people on the same nights so we could come "home" to each other, our fingers smelling like the sex of other people. I found that there was nothing in the world that turned me on more than tasting another woman on his face after reuniting. I was ravenous for him after he went out with someone else in a way few people understood. But he did. And that was all that mattered. Jake's was the kind of love that made me feel safe, enabling me to push and pull in equal measure. If I didn't like something, I said so and so did he. Communication made it possible to experiment with different types of people and scenarios. Sometimes we pushed it too far and we'd have to redefine our boundaries, but it always resulted in a deeper closeness and better understanding of ourselves and each other.

When you are afraid of someone, you cannot tell them what you want and how you feel. But when you're with someone who makes you feel safe . . .

"This is intimacy," he told me, as if I needed to learn. Because I did. No faked feelings. No holding back. For the first time in my life—emotionally, sexually, spiritually—I was able to let go. On our own terms, we had created a relationship that was *as* defined by our security in ourselves as it was with each other. Our desire for others could exist without envy. We had built a world where supporting each other's explorations, together and separately, was the deepest expression of love.

There was no turning back.

———

Despite the sexual openness and honesty, it takes me another two months before I allow myself to hold Jake's hand in public. *I'm not really into PDA* is my excuse. And that is true. But more than that, I'm paranoid that someone will see us—a neighbor or one of Hal's coworkers or someone who once read my blog. That a parent at school will say something to my kids or I will have to answer questions I don't have the answers to. Questions I will receive daily as soon as I go public with this, or any, relationship.

Love, much like grief, is so often complicated by outsiders' expectations. Is that why so many of us perform? Pretend we're not dating when we are and say that we're grieving when we're not? Is this why my social circle shrank after Hal died, even after everyone was so lovely and caring and generous? Why is it that the very community who rallied around us for months and months became the same people I was afraid to be truthful with?

Was it because I assumed that they were supporting a version of me that they wanted to see? That all of the people who so generously sent meals and money to a GoFundMe account a friend started might want to know if their investments were sound? That I wasn't gallivanting off with lovers like a maniac? That I was actually quite practical, chaste, checking off all the good widow boxes?

What kind of woman was I, anyway? The kind they would regret supporting? The kind they would regret sending condolences to? And would they be right?

In those months after Hal died, so many people came and then went. Got close enough to the proverbial casket to view the body and then disappeared. I learned as much from these losses as I did from the friends who became lifelines—the women I bonded with so profoundly in the wake of Hal's death that I became eternally theirs. Matching tattoos on our bodies to remind us of our love. These women created a haven for me and, within the embrace of their nonjudgment and unconditional support, I was able to practice my truths so that, eventually, I could bring them all out into the open. So that in time, the public performance could end, and people would forget I was ever anything other than this.

One day I will run into an acquaintance at the grocery store. I will know by the way her body slumps forward how this will go. How *this* always goes. I'll be somewhere in pubic and someone will see me and...

"Oh, honey," she'll say, teary-eyed—her arms outstretched. "I'm so sorry."

And then she will surround me with her body—tell me that she can't believe I lost my soul mate. She will say so many things to me assuming that she knows. She will be one of dozens of people who mean well without knowing what they mean.

Which is why I will finally say something in front of the watermelons.

"Please don't be sorry for me. For him, yes. But not for me. I'm okay. I'm actually really happy."

And she will say nothing—smile at me but barely. Let me go.

Later that evening, I will hold Jake's hand as we walk down Wilshire. And then I will kiss him in front of my house just as my neighbors are coming home from work.

It is as pubic a display as I can think of.

A love parade.

———

As soon as Jake and I become serious, I tell my kids that I will continue to casually date and so will he. I explain that this is what I want right now.

That I deserve to feel safe and happy in a relationship that makes me feel both of those things.

"I am trying to create my own version of a partnership that prioritizes my wants and needs—my truth. Experimenting."

"We are all wired differently. And it's important to me to honor myself and be honest with you about who I am."

Months into Jake's and my relationship, I make plans to take a woman to dinner. We date sporadically over the next several months, but in order to meet her the first time, I call Jake to see if he can cover for the babysitter who has just called in sick.

"Of course," he tells me. "I'm impressed that you asked."

I am not good at asking for help, and the thought of asking Jake to look after my kids while I date someone else seems like it might be crossing a line—it would be for most people—but we are not most people and I am reminded of that when he tells me he *feels fine about it, I'll be right over, go have fun* . . .

"Who are you going out with?" My kids ask.

"A very cool woman. Funny. Smart. Great style."

"Do you like each other?"

"I think so. Yes. We're meeting to see how much."

Weeks later, my kids and I are watching *Mrs. America*, an FX biopic about the women's liberation movement. We watch as Brenda, played by Ari Graynor, confesses to her husband that she has fallen for a woman and they decide to open their marriage.

"Look!" one of my daughters says. "She's just like you!"

"That's right!" I say, snapping my fingers in solidarity. "I kind of think maybe a lot of people are, but we're not supposed to talk about it. Especially to our children."

"But not you, right?"

She holds up her hand and I slap it five.

"No shame, baby."

———

Months into our relationship, Jake began writing tiny little love notes on paper towels.

They all said: *I love you, Be.*

He put them in strange places for me to find. Under my laptop. In my underwear drawer. In the bathroom medicine cabinet. Between folded towels. I find them every now and then and immediately call for the kids in the other room.

"Look at this! I found another one!"

I don't take Jake's notes down. Not even when we break up. Because even in the afterward of our relationship, I know that I deserve the kind of love I always wanted—the kind that feels like freedom. In the end, he gave me a beginning. He called me by a name that described my completeness as someone who existed on her own volition.

I love you, Be.

I love you. Be.

Be

Two months into quarantine, Jake and I make our breakup official while sitting face-to-face, cross-legged on my bed holding hands, my kids voices bouncing off the walls outside my bedroom door.

He has done nothing to deserve my sudden instinct to detach. One day I wake up and realize I cannot be depended on by anyone outside of my children. *My nuclear family does not include him.* The ship is going down. *Women and children first.*

I tell him the truth, callous as it sounds. Life is too claustrophobic right now to be loved, to love back. I have too many mouths to feed, here, in my home. I have nothing left to give. Even good men need too much.

Being around a gentle man for an entire year in the wake of a volatile marriage brought me back to myself. But breaking up with him as soon as I felt I needed space—as opposed to faking my way through something that didn't feel right anymore—meant that I could also self-advocate. Something I had spent years struggling to do.

There is nothing wrong with loving someone and letting them go. Just be.

Part Three

Chapter 19

Witches

I could have started this book with a birthday party. The one I was supposed to have the week after Hal's diagnosis in the same cemetery where we would, months later, bury his remains.

For my thirty-seventh birthday, I wanted to surround myself with the women in my life who had replaced my husband as the relationship I turned to for support. *What's up, ride-or-dies? This is the year I hit the road.* We would gather in the darkness at Hollywood Forever's Cinespia, eat snacks and watch Thelma and Louise break free from their miserable lives. Big screen. Night sky. All wine and women, surrounded by graves and revenge.

In the subject of my email invitation, I quoted Thelma and Louise's *The Ballad of Lucy Jordan.*

*At the age of thirty-seven she realized she'd never ride
through Paris in a sports car with the warm wind in her hair . . .*

My kind of love stories were the ones about women revving the engines of Ford Thunderbirds, joining hands and breaking free. So I changed the lyric, spiked it with hope:

At the age of thirty-seven she realized she could STILL ride
through Paris in a sports car with the warm wind in her hair..."

The morning Hal was admitted to the hospital, I canceled my birthday party and broke the news of his diagnosis in the same email thread. And then my girlfriends, many of them strangers to each other, teamed up and went to war.

I will never know the extent of what they did for me in the days, weeks, and months that followed. They took me off the thread and created their own committee overnight. And from there, people just started showing up to help. Every day. With no end in sight. Because of them, I thrived in spite of the chaos. So did my children. Our extended family. Everyone.

These women organized cancer walks and meal trains, bar mitzvahs and GoFundMes. They swept through our home with cleaning supplies, flowers, and strong arms to move furniture to make way for hospital beds. They held me up, brushed my hair, brought me food, and made me feel like I was a part of a greater female entity. That I was one in a long line of women being carried by her coven.

Light as a feather stiff as a board but only because of all the hands that lifted me up—a well-oiled machine of love and organization, made possible by the women I called to gather with me in celebration amongst the dead.

My love for women—as friends—was not a love I came to on my own. At eighteen and throughout my early twenties, I lived almost exclusively with men and the majority of my time, up until my marriage, was spent living, working, dating and partying with dudes. I was "a girl's guy." You know, just one of the boys. In my midtwenties, I even went so far as to call myself a *masculinist*. I believed a woman's sexual power to be far superior than the cultural power men wielded, convinced that, because men were unable to control their urges, women must hold all the cards.

Isn't that why we're taught as teenage girls that men can't control themselves? That it's our fault we are so irresistible. Hypnotic. Sirens calling upon the sailors, luring them into the depths with our voices. *I guess they have no choice but to touch us in the places they don't understand.*

I have been one of many to chastise feminist fathers for claiming that the birth of their daughters awakened their own feminism, but, the truth is, it wasn't until I gave birth to my first daughter that I considered myself a feminist, too. And while I realize now that having a vagina does not mean she would identify as girl, I felt a corporeal surge in the depth of me the moment I pushed my second child out from between my legs and heard her scream.

How does a mother bring a daughter into the world without wanting to change it? The moment we locked eyes, I was radicalized. If I could not protect her from the world, I would teach myself to fight it.

———

We learn the power of stories at an early age. Our parents kiss us on our foreheads and tuck us in with the promises of happy endings. Of hope springing eternal in whatever afters. *Everything is going to be okay,* they tell us, and we have to believe them because, why would they lie? This sort of one-size-fits-all narrative arc is soothing, like a back scratch at bedtime. *Okay, then. Go to sleep now. Goodnight.* We learn who we're supposed to be this way, which is very different from who we actually are.

We line our dolls up in neat rows and press teacups to sealed lips, their wide marble eyes staring intently at us as we kill them off and then bring them back to life. Give them second chances. Speak for them with frilly accents, low-pitched howls.

I recently read that the traditional three-act story structure with climax and denouement is reflective of the male orgasm. Which makes sense since climaxing, for men, is the heart of fucking. But that isn't true for most women. It isn't for me. I am far more interested in the story behind the sex, the setting and characters—all of the ways we strip down to nothing before entering each other's bodies. Pleasure, of course, is the point. But so is its proximity to everything else. To truth and discovery, opening up and letting go.

In the beginning, I only knew what I was taught. Told. Read. I was shy in public until I learned by trial and error with my Barbies how to be cool enough to be accepted into The Dreamhouse. If my instincts opposed whatever story I had been told, I ignored them. Buried them in diaries with plastic padlocks. Kept them to myself, ashamed of my darkness, of stories with more than one ending.

I learned to arc a story the same way I learned to arc my body—how to write a climax and how to cause one. It was never about me so much as the structure of the thing. The beginning, middle, and end. It wasn't until years later I realized that where a man often ends, a woman begins.

In life as it is in death as it is in orgasms.

"Don't move. I'm still coming."

As a girl, I was taught to be a woman by learning the narrative structures of men. And all these years later, I am still unlearning.

What kind of story only climaxes once?

Not mine.

The first person I confess my true feelings to is Erica.

My first cousin on my mother's side, Erica and I grew up a mile from each other. We went to school together, just one year apart. The first time I shaved my legs was in her bathtub and my entire sexual awakening was predicated on the fact that she had Showtime at her house, thus making it impossible not to watch *Red Shoe Diaries* for hours at a time in the safety of the guest bedroom, volume on three.

"Eww," we would collectively groan, "this is disgusting."

But we never turned it off.

Instead, we peeked from between the same hands we used to shield our eyes. Dumbstruck by the sexual depravity of a garter belt, the demonstrativeness of a slowly loosened bow tie.

And then, when we'd had enough of that, we'd tell secrets in the darkness and scratch each other's backs until we fell asleep.

Our back scratches were called *colors* and consisted of a "scratch option menu," with a rainbow of options to choose from. Pick three.

Red was hard scratches, the kind that left marks. Orange was soft, gentle. Like a tickle. Yellow was massage. Green was karate chops. Blue was a sort of kneading. Purple was little pounds. We both always picked the same three. Red, orange, and yellow.

Back and forth. My hands against her back and then hers against mine.

Erica flew down at various times when Hal was sick and in the weeks and months that came after. It was as if she knew exactly when to find me. Like she could anticipate my need for her, knowing that I was never going to be a person who asked. Like my friends, she just showed up.

Because she *knew*. Because, magic.

One night, as we're lying in the bed I once shared with Hal, Erica asks what colors I want her to draw on my back. It's been twenty years since we've done this. Maybe even twenty-five, but I instantly know what colors I'm going to pick and, suddenly, I am nine years old again and full of secrets.

"Erica. I have to tell you something . . ."

She listens. Her fingernails soft against my back. Orange.

". . . I'm glad he's gone . . ."

She draws circles on my back. Up my shoulders. Down my side and around my waist.

". . . I didn't want him to die but I'm so relieved he isn't here . . ."

I can feel her nodding. Listening. Her soft scratches becoming yellow, a massage.

I have opened the wound to release the pressure and now the guts are everywhere.

". . . I don't know what to call this feeling . . . but I feel so relieved."

She scratches harder now. Knowing exactly where to scratch at what itches, what ails.

"How can a person feel relieved that her husband is gone?"

She draws lines and then more lines. And then triangles across my back. Big ones then little ones and then circles again. Spirals . . .

". . . Even just saying those words aloud feels cruel . . . Am I a terrible person?"

"No," she says, "you are a person."

We stay up most of the night in my bed like we did as children and I tell her every truth I have spent the last few months feeling. And she listens and tells me she loves me *and it's okay, I understand.*

When I wake up, she is gone. She's on an airplane back to San Francisco, but on her side of the bed, she leaves a note.

You deserve to feel EVERYTHING, it says.

What if we all spoke truthfully about our feelings and experiences? What if we weren't afraid of being chastised for our humanity? What if, we felt safe enough to open the parts of ourselves we have been culturally conditioned to keep closed—didn't have to call each other brave for saying the things we know to be true, and instead of *protecting our families* from knowing our pain, allowed them to understand what we risk by saying nothing.

So many of us say nothing. Raise our daughters to say nothing. Send the message to our sons, that no matter what they do to us—we will say nothing.

———

On Archer's fifteenth birthday, I sit him down under the moon at midnight and surround him with his sisters. My friend Veronika is here, too, and we all hold candles. We bless him with the life force of a million unhatched eggs. Five of us around him like a pentagram, a symbol as commonly misunderstood as the witches who swear by its elements. A mother, her daughters, and her best friend. We talk about living in a commune when this is all over. A coven. Sharing a space. Romantic love is not for me, maybe. Or perhaps it is, but it will look like something else. A story seldom told or not at all. The kind of fairy tale we should have always told our children, where *witches* aren't villains and women aren't victims and the heroes on horseback aren't men.

That's right. This time our stories will be told in braids. Loosely overlapping and free at the ends. Redorangeyellow down our backs.

There is magic in the breaking of spells.

CHAPTER 20

Sirens

I once compared my marriage to going to the beach and not wearing sunscreen. I have done this a hundred times even though I know I will burn. Some people tan and part of me believes I will, too. That the burning is something I can outgrow. That, with age, I'll toughen up. But every time I lie in the sun, I burn. Even if it's just a few minutes. That's just the kind of skin I have. Hereditarily pale. Sensitive.

Every time I get sunburned, I become unreasonably angry with myself and the whole world. Especially my mother, whose skin I inherited. And then, days later, the discomfort will disappear, and I forget how painful it is to have blisters on my shoulders. I look almost tan and marvel at my deepened shade. I feel beautiful. And then, in the morning, my skin falls off like scales. It flakes into the cups of my bra and for the next few days I pick skin out from under my fingernails. The itch of a momentary glow.

One cannot change her skin's constitution. I explain this to my children, two of whom burn like me. Tough girls still burn.

The problem with marrying someone you don't know very well is that it's impossible to know if, once the sheen of lust has subsided, your love will be compatible. For years, I thought it was worth the burn to have a day or two of tan. But when your marriage is mainly char and itch, the beauty that lives momentarily strung between these two forms of violence begins to look like something else. This kind of molting is unnatural—a redness that blanches when pressed, that keeps you up at all hours cradling a bottle of aloe.

Paradoxically, the beauty of being in a challenging relationship of any kind is the years spent worshipping and cursing the same warmth. Anything with the capacity to give life can also take it away. The sun heals with the same breath that it burns, nourishes with the same heat that starves. But just because our tissues know how to scar, doesn't mean we should excuse that which has disfigured us.

Culturally, women have made it a point to ignore the faults and foibles of men posthumously. We have pretended bad marriages were good. Made excuses for abusive behavior at the expense of our own safety, gaslighting ourselves into oblivion. Out of fear, denial, patriarchy. *There are so many reasons to stay*, we explain to ourselves in the shower. Or on the car ride home from school drop off. Or in bed, unable to sleep. But none of those reasons involve our happiness. Not directly.

For many of us, the ease with which we learn to lie is what keeps us safe in a profoundly unsafe world. Pretending we love it here. That everything's just fine, thank you. *Look at me smile I am so happy. I love my life. I love my life. I love my life.* We tell ourselves stories as protection, as a way to harden our softness, and from there learn to outwardly thrive.

It's so much easier to do nothing than it is to fight back.

But just because we can succeed in spite of our wounds does not mean they haven't also crippled us. My mother burned just like I did and one day woke up with cancer spots all over her skin, which she now must have removed every year or so. The long-term effects of thinking we can handle all the things that we cannot are profound. A pale girl without protection cannot survive that much sun.

I wear sunscreen now. Most of the time, anyway. One can only take so many years of burning in order to tan. But now and then, I'm like, *fuck this! I don't feel like wearing sunscreen!* And every time, I'm handed the same reminder in the throbbing vermillion of blistered shoulders—you cannot teach old skin new tricks.

Blisters eventually pop like little volcanoes, revealing newer, more supple skin. It is through a woman's most traumatized openings that new life has always begun.

One day I wake up and I'm not angry.

I wish I knew why. That there were instructions I could pass on for letting go. A secret sauce with ingredients from an old family recipe. But we don't work that way, do we? I certainly don't. I have always felt as if I was inexplicably wired to feel and then not feel. To love and then not love. *The wind changed*: that's always been my explanation.

One day I wake up and feel a space in my body where the anger used to be. Like a hunger pang but in reverse. Perhaps it took writing this book. Getting through the earlier chapters. Telling all of the stories I had kept to myself. Perhaps a part of him was still with me. The part I needed to fight off. To get angry with. And maybe I did it. Got it all out. Everything I needed to say. Maybe I just needed to get up and walk around instead of trying to sleep when I wasn't tired.

Days later, after appealing to a new sense of self, recognizing a sort of closure that wasn't there before, and feeling for the first time that perhaps Hal's spirit had moved on and so had I, I come home to my house after dropping the kids off at school, place my keys on the entry table, and promptly collapse.

It started as heartburn earlier that morning—a pain deep in the back of my chest. And now it's pounding like fists. My whole body is vibrating. I can feel it in my arms and my legs.

I am an earthquake.

"Someone come quick," I say, but I am alone.

Should I call an ambulance?

I hold onto my heart, waiting for it to pass. Nothing has triggered this, so all I can think is that . . . something has found its way back into the anger nook. The space where the hunger wasn't. This pain I feel is unfamiliar, maybe because these are the feelings everyone expected me to have. Suddenly I feel . . . unimaginably sad.

My breath catches in my throat and I can't breathe. I am the San Andreas after the shaking has stopped. My fault lines are relieved. I am still.

It has passed, yes, but only the earthquake.

And now I have remembered my oceans. That I am more water than land.

A wave must be coming.

———

I came of age in the ocean, swimming past the break with my friends, all mermaids. We were barely teenagers, but we knew where we were going. When you're young, you remember your wild. You know innately that, contrary to the warnings of adults with check-ered flags, the farther you swim from the shore, the safer you are from the curl of the waves. And so on hot summer days we would paddle out with salty hair, hold our noses against whitewash until we reached the liquid glass. Together, we would float on our backs. Yank at the strings on our bikinis until they were loose enough to pull off our chests with two fingers. For minutes, we'd be naked in the depths of the ocean. Safely tucked behind the waves. No break behind us to look out for. No surprises.

From the depths, we would watch the waves appear like a simulation. Waves look so much smaller when watching them roll in from behind. Like little hills in our periphery as we paddled half naked, flipping our tails under water as the fists of foam rolled violently on to shore.

People spoke of sharks and riptides and the dangers of getting stuck *way out there in the depths*, but it never happened to any of us. Adults had their warnings and we had our wings. Our strings. Our scales.

When people talk about grief and how it *comes in waves*, this is what I think about. I think about what it felt like before I knew that the adults were telling the truth. I think about being thirteen and fourteen and fifteen. When my body still felt like mine alone. I think about taking off my bikini top and floating in the sun.

I remember the feeling that *even when I felt safe, I knew the waves were there*. I could not stay beyond them forever. I would have to be prepared for them to take me under. I would have to hold my breath, and swim. But first, I had to learn to be still. To lean into the movement. To let go.

Swimming is dangerous when you're afraid to float.

I try to explain this to the people I love who want to do something and feel hopeless when they can't. I want to tell them it's like trying to save someone from drowning while standing on the sand. Like telling someone who cannot hold her breath under water to *swim, swim to shore*.

"It must be so hard," people say.

"Yes, thank you," I say back.

I want them to understand that the sadness I feel isn't solely because of the death. It's because of the way he died. The way we ended. The way we were. I am grieving the fourteen years I spent in a marriage I knew wasn't right for me. I am grieving for all the ways I created stories to convince myself this was the life I signed up for. I am grieving for all of the women who are currently doing the same.

Some of us don't want to be comforted. We don't want advice or a friend to hold our hand. We want to be left alone. We want to break down until we remember our breath. We want to wait until nightfall for everyone to go home, swim back to shore on our own time, under the light of the moon.

———

There's this scene in *Mermaids* where Cher is dancing around the kitchen with her daughters. She, like me, hates to cook, but also like me (ha!), it's part of her charm.

Her youngest daughter tells her older sister, "I think I heard Mom saying she was going to make a main course tonight" as in, she made ACTUAL dinner as opposed to, you know, the usual appetizers and snacks.

The moment the words leave her lips, Cher appears, clutching a pink paper bag. She smiles and pulls out a yellow dress, dancing past them as they look at each other.

"Nah," they say.

In this moment they are acknowledging something profound—that not all mothers are the same. Some mothers would rather dance around a kitchen than cook in one. And *their* mother—even if she's not like other mothers—is the only mother they need.

I am watching this scene with all three of my daughters. They take their eyes off the screen and look at me, and I pop up from where I'm wedged between them and start dancing on the bed to the same song.

"If you want to be happy for the rest of your life never make a pretty woman your wife."

The girls join me. We're dancing around my bedroom, candles

as microphones, middle fingers extended toward the voices as they croon, *"She's ugly but she sure can cook!"*

BOOOOOOOOOOOO!

The volume is at full blast and I fucking love it. We're all commotion and dirty socks, incense, and noise. No one can tell me to turn down the volume. No one can tell me what to watch with my daughters at midnight in the summertime.

No one can tell me I'm singing too loud.

The girls flop around on my bed. "Look! We're like mermaids, too."

And they are.

And we are.

And I am.

Behind us, the credits roll. No rush to get back to the shore.

Chapter 21

Everyone Is a Storm/April 2020

It's April no-one-knows-what-day-it-is-anymore, a month after the schools have all closed down. All of the children are home and we're supposed to teach them with someone else's lesson books. The world is ending again, a lesson that continues throughout the various and unexpected turns of mortal life. The world will end a little bit every day until we do. That is the nature of being in a human body on this planet. That is the nature of being awake knowing that, come midnight, we will seek out our caskets, lie down, and disappear.

My oldest two are in Zoom classrooms, adapting to their new normal without my guidance. Archer is almost fifteen and Fable will be twelve in the fall. But the little ones are only eight and in second grade and their lesson plans are as scattered as I am.

"Just do your best," I say, combing their tangled hair with my fingers. "You have all the answers."

We're supposed to know what to do with math equations where the rules have changed so drastically that addition reads more like subtraction. It reminds me of how every generation gets it wrong. *No, we don't. Yes, you do. Yes, we don't. No, we do.*

When my children are adults, their children will do math in

a different way, too. They will stand over the shoulders of their daughters whispering numbers to themselves in hopes a solution will come tumbling out of some divine well, or maybe they'll just ask Alexa and Siri for help. Maybe there will be no such thing as math class because all of the answers will become even more accessible and school will render itself obsolete. Then again, I thought this would be the case by now. When I was a child in school, I never understood why we spent so much time learning about things we didn't need to know when I had so many questions about life—about real life—that went unanswered. Unstudied. Unlearned.

———

While Hal lay dying, the California wildfires blazed—smoke billowing from east and west, north and south. It was the deadliest, most destructive wildfire season on record in California.

When I took the kids up to Oregon after Hal's service in mid-November, many of the fires were still going. We watched LA fade into the distance from the view of the airplane, heartbroken that so much below us had burned. And then, a few months later, the rain started and it seemed as if it would never stop. The roof leaked in three places. We kept losing power. The streets flooded. No one could stop talking about the rain. For the five of us, it felt like some kind of relief to put pots under the holes in the ceiling. Like maybe the sky understood. The old walls, too.

After the rains, we drove to the poppy reserve. We go every year, but this time was different. The hills were alive, painted with orange blossoms all along the highway. None of us could believe our eyes.

That's when we talked about the wildfires and record rains, the flooding and the leaks, the ash that fell from the sky and didn't stop. *And then one day you wake up and the hills are all in bloom. They don't even look real. Nothing is on fire anymore. Some days you forget there even was a fire. The rain is gone. And everywhere you look there are flowers.*

———

There is a worldwide pandemic and I am my children's only living parent. And this is supposed to make me feel scared. I know it is because people keep asking me how I deal with my anxiety and fear of the unknown and I tell them that I don't have either of those things and for a while I believe it's true. After six months, though, this changes. I reach my breaking point, walk calmly into the kitchen and, one at a time, throw every dirty dish from the sink onto the floor. My children, startled by the sound of shattering bowls, stand with mouths agape and I say nothing to explain. Instead, I let my hands do the talking. This is what I'm supposed to be doing right now. They can stay and watch if they want to, but I will not pretend to be okay. Not even for them. I nod, as if to salute them, my witnesses. This is what it feels like to be a mother right now. Everything I feel sounds like the breaking of plates. Of bowls. Of plastic glasses that, I now know, can shatter, too, when thrown hard enough against tile floor. Smash. Smash. Smash.

I break them all until there is nothing left in the sink but a yellow sponge. Hundreds of tiny pieces around me. I'm relieved and panting, standing in the middle of it all.

Later, I sit down with my children and explain what just happened. I tell them how hard it's been trying to write about our first world war while standing in the wreckage of the second. That I am not unbreakable. That I will eventually shatter when pushed far enough. Break into three hundred pieces. Maybe not the first time I'm thrown, but eventually.

Sometimes the only way to stand firmly on the precipice of a new life is to simulate the crumbling of another.

"I need a break, you guys."

I need to break.

Make the movement through the rubble tangible. Pick up the pieces. Now let them go.

When Hal was sick, I had a recurring dream that there was a flood. I was washing dishes in a log cabin somewhere in the forest. I even had an apron on. It was holiday-movie inspired. I was chunky sweater-clad, humming quietly, gazing out the window at the peaceful and seemingly impenetrable woods. That's when I noticed the water in the distance pouring down the mountain. But before I had time to react it was already inside the house. I held my breath, looked for my kids underwater but couldn't find them. Not until I reached land did they appear, one by one. Each one saving themselves.

It was like Bo's picture. The one from before with the fire and the open eyes.

Hal was never in these dreams. Even after he died, I waited for him to find me. But in two years of dreaming, he only came to me once.

"Does anyone want to write with me?" I call out one morning. Bo says yes, dirty fingers wrapped around the Chromebook I will have to send back for repairs three times in four months.

She sits down beside me and starts typing. "A book," she tells me. "About a girl who is the most powerful element in the world."

The girl is fourteen years old and unafraid of the evil wizard who lives underground. She knows he's there but goes on various missions anyway. She is afraid in the way people are afraid when they know that their power is greater than their fear. Her name is Olivia, but she pronounces it oh-live-yah.

Oh.

Live.

Yeah.

She sends me what she writes as she's writing and my phone vibrates with notifications, a thread of reminders to be brave and powerful and okay with being afraid.

Meanwhile, her twin sister sleeps on my knees. She doesn't want to write and I don't blame her. It feels impossibly difficult to do so right now. Where does one even begin? When you're stuck inside an experience, it's hard to describe the way it looks on the outside. It's hard to remember the color of the sky.

Revie lies with her face against her hands, so dry from washing. Over and over she washes them, even when she doesn't have to. This is nothing new. She started washing her hands raw in preschool. Now, I rub lotion on them every morning and plead with her not to use so much soap next time.

"But everyone says . . ."

"Ignore them," I tell her.

"But what about the germs?"

A blue scrub jay builds a nest outside my window. She pulls twigs from living trees with easy snaps. I watch her fold her wings against her body and disappear beneath the arch of our tile roof. All she needs to know to build a nest is that it's spring.

The clicking of my laptop keys wakes Revie. Slowly, she opens her eyes. She knows I am writing about her father and about me and all the ways I have changed since the death. And I want to tell her everything and nothing. I don't want her to make the same mistakes I did but I also want her to know I have never regretted the life I chose that brought me here. I want her to remember her father with love and also truth. *Rather than love, than money, than fame, give me truth.*

Outside a streak of blue ascends and we watch her disappear together, hands clasped.

"I think she probably left to get more sticks," Revie says about the bird.

"I think you're probably right."

Nests don't build themselves.

CHAPTER 22

Bylines

The day Danielle reached out to me wasn't the first time.

Our bylines had brushed up against each other for nearly a decade. She was a writer, too—an essayist who wrote editorials about motherhood for the same publications I did, our children's early milestones rooted to the same HTML. *Mommy bloggers*, they called us. Our names, faces, and stats listed on tear sheets sent out to sponsorships—agents pitching us together for the same campaigns. We wrote for the same websites but never met in person, our homes on opposite sides of the country. Occasionally, we would locate each other's avatars in the threads of comments sections, tip our hats in solidarity. *I just love you*, we would say to each other. *Girl, same.*

Like me, she wrote about the mess. About being flawed and human and frustrated and a little bit fucked up. She was punk rock the way early blogging was punk rock. Pre Influencer. When you could curse in sponsored posts and share photos without filters. Our voices were all we needed and brands came to us, not to dilute what we were writing, but to capitalize on the audiences we had amassed by becoming one-women enterprises. The term *mommy-blogger* has since been relegated to a sort of punchline, but women like Danielle and me were integral voices in a space that expanded because of the work we did on an internet that was still finding its footing in the mid-aughts. We were mothers of a movement that outgrew us, the doors we opened hitting us in the face on the way out. But for years, we were able to capitalize on our voices. Our stories and seasons and signs. For nearly a decade, we made enough money to support our families as writers on websites we maintained and ran ourselves.

I stopped monetizing my blog when it stopped being worth it and started freelancing, instead. Danielle did the same, getting a nine-to-five job before quitting her blog entirely with a name change and a buzzer to the scalp two weeks before Hal's death.

I watched the video of her shaving her head over and over. Watched her cry, her hair falling down her body in long blonde strands, the slashing of a feminine power which, for years, had contributed to her feelings of powerlessness. The paradox of beauty and all its trappings. The relief of disappearing years of trauma in the growth that fell to the ground after spending years as weight on her shoulders. A *Mormon girl* who escaped. A *wife* who walked out. The kind of beauty that cannot be unseen, even when it doesn't come close to the brilliance of the brain that inhabits it.

She dropped her ex-husband's name at the same time. Her father's last name, too.

Fuck a maiden name. She was a woman whose legacy would be her own. I was in awe.

There is nothing more beautiful than a middle-aged woman who isn't afraid to start over. To clear the wreckage and say to the world, *This is me, brand new.* And grow again.

A woman unlearning is the most powerful kind. Perhaps that was why I could not look away from her. I didn't want to. I direct messaged her and told her how much she meant to me. That even though we'd never met, I knew. That watching her was my own catharsis. That her vulnerability reminded me to trust my own.

"I understand," is what I told her.

"I've been thinking of you," is what she said back.

We exchanged numbers that day—two women grieving past lives becoming new.

"I see you."

"I see you, too."

In *On Lies, Secrets, and Silence* Adrienne Rich writes, "Women have often felt insane when cleaving to the truth of experience. Our future depends on the sanity of each of us and we have a profound stake, beyond the personal, in the project of describing our reality as candidly and fully as we can to each other."

———

Danielle and I check in with each other sporadically over the next two years, mainly with comments on each other's Instagram posts. And then she hears me on a podcast in the early months of quarantine and reaches out via text. It starts with talk of open relationships—of hers and mine and how, after her marriage went bad, she would never do monogamy again. We relate to each other's experiences on many things, the ease of our correspondence turns into a sort of rapid-fire compliment-fest until she asks *if I am flirting with her* and I tell her *yes, I am.*

Just like that, I have struck a match against her friction and *boom.* We go from friends to lovers within hours. Our texts like fingers slowly undressing, our paragraphs voracious, emanating with longing, houses on fire.

We confess through the boxes of our iPhones to having held crushes on each other for years. We are on our knees hailing Mother Mary, not in repentance, but in revelation. Her religious upbringing had shamed her for her sexuality since childhood, but here she is, standing with me, middle fingers extended toward the church she left many times, only to become more and more herself.

If we could have found a Mormon church to fuck in that first night, we would have. Instead, we build our own altar and make each other come against its carpet with our commas. Pulling on our own hair with long-distance hands.

Together, we take the pieces of our pasts and flip them over, matching our truths against each other like a game of Memory. Scars so similar, it would be hard to know which one belonged to whom. *I have that one, too.*

With her, I am undone—under new rule, everything is different. It feels as if our paths have been crossing since before we were even born, like we are extensions of each other. Reunited after years of separation, retracing our steps through a parallel universe—landing each day in a haven of unprecedented understanding.

All it takes is two women to break one gaslight in the square. This is how rebellions start.

We braid our hair together knowing the third strand is a life we will never inhabit. It is our separation that brings us together. If we don't speak for days at a time, it is only because we don't need to keep track of each other. Like mothers who let their children run free in the rain, knowing they grow best that way. Our stems bend toward each other because they can't touch. We find each other like teenage girls with flashlights beaming from two different time zones, our windows cloudy with the relief of our exhales. Even though our bodies are strangers. Another pair of distanced lovers tucked away on separate balconies, slowly growing our hair.

"I feel like you found me while I was finding myself and there is so much power in that."

———

When all you have are words, you can have it all if you say so. You can forge your own path through the clearing with the light from the same moon. Spend the night together while in two separate houses. Even with men in your beds. You can write your own love story, defiant of genre, of timeline, of page.

———

Danielle understood me. She understood my grief and also my relief. She understood what I was still having a hard time saying out loud. She read my words and sent them back oxygenated with her understanding.

"You had to mourn inside a box that you did not fit into and you had to present all of these faces for everyone and keep it together for your kids . . . I can only imagine how hard that must have been."

"I feel like there's no going back now. That I would become violent in a love story where a man would ask anything of me at all. Hal's death robbed me of feeling like I could hate him."

"That sentence goes in your book."

It was impossible to know if the intensity of our affair was predicated on the fact that it was, for both of us, a first. While we had experienced women sexually in our pasts, we had never felt this kind of woman-to-woman pull. Would we have found each other eventually? Would we have even known where to begin if it wasn't for our matching pasts? I think of all the unhappily married couples and women who love women in secret. All of their undiscovered islands. Danielle made me want to break all of these women free so that they could find each other and feel seen.

Think of all the undiscovered harbors and all the boats that will never make it to shore.

In many ways, it was like losing our virginity all over again. Finding new ways to reach each other and touch each other and to relate to each other long distance. It felt as though I was redoing every milestone. First steps and first words and first day of school. Loving a woman for the first time made me feel like I was doing love all wrong—until now.

"I think we both use words as shields, and I want to remove them from our mouths so we can get lost in each other."

We were a paradise of desperately romantic clichés—twins separated at birth, retracing our steps. How could we have possibly lived without each other—without this—for all these years?

"This is a new feeling. I am shifting on a cellular level. I can feel my brain rewiring."

"You are leading the way to an existence I didn't think was possible. By being yourself, you have shown me the way."

———

We spend three months corresponding by phone and packaged gifts. We film hour-long videos for each other on Marco Polo, confessing our love to each other while walking our dogs through Pennsylvania fields (her) and Los Angeles intersections (me). We send each other books to read together and flowers to display in our separate bedrooms and countless personal gifts with messaging in languages only we can understand.

We play each other music and talk about all the yesterdays it took to give us today. We don't talk of tomorrow. There is no tomorrow.

We both have lived enough lives to know that everything we need is here. That all we need are our bodies and the children who stretched and then deflated our wombs—who crawl in and out of our beds as we dream of each other in all the ways we are other than mother.

My bedroom becomes filled with souvenirs of our romance. My phone, a paper trail of confessions—our two-way diary.

———

"I think about how fast we caught fire. How we were made of kindling all these years and just needed a light. How after years of bad marriages and writing between the lines of truth and all the ways we postured to survive, we both had to die to come back. And in coming back, we found each other at the precise moment we were ready to be found, wandering in the same clearing with open eyes."

There's a mirror to us, yes. But, also, something else—a kind of love that exists as something inexplicably tied to the finding and building of a new foundation with someone who is just as unfamiliar with the materials. Suddenly there are no limitations on what love can look like. Or our stories.

———

I decide to buy a plane ticket and fly to Pennsylvania to see her. In early October, seven months into a global pandemic. Family testing plus quarantine plus long weekend at my parents' house, so that I, desperately in love and impossibly selfish, can spend a long weekend away to see about a girl.

As soon as I board the plane, I immediately feel guilty. *What am I doing on an airplane? We don't even know each other. How could I leave my children at a time like this? Is this who I am?* And the answer, of course, is yes. Yes, this is who I am. I am the kind of woman who gets on an airplane to meet someone I only know from a distance, during a time when being distanced is all we are supposed to be. Because while I can obey almost every pandemic rule, this is the one I am willing to break. Because who the fuck knows what will come next. Maybe this is it! Maybe all we have is this moment. What happens if it passes and so do we?

Living in proximity to death will either make you more afraid of dying or detached from its heaviness. I realize on the airplane, flipping through in-flight entertainment, that I am, in this moment, of the latter category. And then I see it. Like a flashing neon sign from the patron saint of cemetery birthday parties, right under Award Winning Classics: *Thelma and Louise.*

My kind of love stories are the ones about women revving the engines of Ford Thunderbirds, joining hands, and breaking free.

I don't get up the entire six-hour flight. I sit against the window in a mask I don't remove until I get into Danielle's minivan and tell her hi, hours before we kiss for the first time on the foot of a bed in a Philadelphia Airbnb.

———

The further I get from loss, the closer I get to understanding what it means to love without consequence. I don't expect longevity. Everything that lives will also die and that includes feelings. Moments. Experiences we share with the people who change our lives.

This is the gift of death. This is the gift of rebirth.

"We made it out, girl. And then we made it in," she says.

Like we've escaped something from two different exits. Like we found each other in the *now what.* And neither of us needs an answer. Feelings are like clouds that change with the *whether.* We are here now and that's enough. May as well lie on our backs and watch rabbits become ships become sky.

On the way home from Philadelphia, I keep my screen turned off. Instead, I listen to the playlists we made each other over the last several months. Joni Mitchell's "Case of You" is on every mix. I replay our weekend and all the ways *we removed words from each other's mouths so that we could get lost in each other.* Like a one-night stand, except ours lasted three days and three nights with no real ending save for a kiss goodbye at the airport.

"Fly safe."

About thirty minutes into *Thelma and Louise*, while driving down an open road in the darkness, Thelma, marveling at the open sky says, "my god, this is beautiful . . . I always wanted to travel. I just never got the opportunity," to which Louise offers a smile and says, "You got it now."

Thelma smiles and closes her eyes as the synthesizer fades in like a heartbeat. This moment right here is the happy ending. It doesn't even matter what happens next.

Together they decided they are free.

CHAPTER 23

Birthdays

On what would have been Hal's forty-sixth birthday, Fable gets a text message on her phone.

"Mama? Someone is looking for Dad . . ."

I gave Fable Hal's phone after he died and sometimes she gets texts for him. Spam, mostly. But occasionally, even now, someone long lost from Hal's past reaches out to see how he's doing. Last year, on what would have been his forty-fifth birthday, there were three people who texted. This year it was only one. Marie. She was his masseuse. I know this because, when I scroll up, I can see that the last time he texted her was in early October 2018 about her availability.

Except it wasn't for him, it was for me.

Hal: *Hey. I was wondering if you had any appointments available this week? For my wife, Bec. She could really use a massage right now.*

Marie: *Sure! Have her text me and we'll set something up?*

Hal: *Great, thanks. I will.*

But he never had me text her and I never set something up. I didn't even know, until now, that he was thinking of me. Not like that.

She could really use a massage right now.

I study the words of this text like some kind of message from the hereafter and wonder if perhaps Hal loved me in a way he was never able to properly articulate.

And that breaks my heart in an entirely new way.

Why was it so hard for us to love each other the way we needed to be loved? Why couldn't he have made me feel seen the way I do now after reading a two-year-old text message? I really could have used a massage.

Birthdays are hard. His. Mine. The kids. As I write this, our children are fifteen, twelve, and nine. They have lived nearly three years without him and have grown into people he will never get to know. Since Hal's death, I have held my breath on every birthday, wedged between guilt and gratitude for the privilege of aging and all that it means to turn over a new year.

For my thirty-ninth birthday, I ask for one gift: alone time in the desert to finish this book. Weeks earlier, I made the realization that I had, paradoxically, spent the entirety of my last two years as a "single" person surrounded by people. My children, of course, but also family, lovers, friends. I even had children climbing into bed with me every night I slept. My space was inhabited at all times except for school hours. But, in quarantine, that ended, too. Solitude was an inaccessible concept.

The last time I spent any real time away by myself was twenty years ago. I was in Europe traveling with my grandmother when I decided to stay behind on my own after she flew back to the states. I was determined to prove myself as a cosmopolitan woman—that, at nineteen years old, I could *do it* on my own.

But the fantasy and the reality were nowhere near the same. I was a teenager alone in a city where I did not know the language and had but one single Parisian acquaintance—the roommate of a friend who agreed to let me stay in the empty room in his apartment for a month, and who *clearly* did not want me there.

The night of my nineteenth birthday, sitting at an outside table at Shakespeare and Company, I ordered a single piece of cake and promptly burst into tears. It was a scene I had dreamt about for years as the perfect setting for a birthday. I would drink espresso and chain smoke in my black dress and *celebrate my independence*! And while that's sort of what I did, I also wrote twenty pages in my journal about how miserable I was and how badly I wanted to end it all and *throw myself into the Seine*!

It was an important lesson—a humbling reminder that for all my posturing as *a certain kind of woman*, I was, in the end, desperate for human connection. That loneliness was a danger I could not handle. I was the kind of girl who turned to darkness when left to her own devices.

This is why I have to go to the desert alone. Relationships have always been my armor. Human bodies an escape. It is also very clear that after two years of human insulation, I need to give myself to the ghosts.

It is time to give up the pacifiers so I can step out into the darkness, breathe it all in, and exhale.

———

The desert was the last place we went as a family, which is why I chose to return. It's very me to want to punctuate a story with a circular motion. I could just see Hal shaking his head at me, like, *wow, Bec. Do you really have to bring it back to the beginning?* And, *yes, I guess I do*. But Joshua Tree wasn't where we began, it was where we ended up—our last trip as a family of six celebrating the start of summer in a little house with a pool and a record player and a freezer we filled with Otter Pops.

I must have taken three hundred pictures of my kids on that trip and, yet, even though Hal was there in the same pool and the same house and on the same sojourn into Pioneertown, he is missing from every image. This was on purpose, of course. I had been erasing him long before he left us. Manifesting a life without him. Cropping him out. And I realize, months later, that in the two years before Hal died, I can count the number of photos I have of him on one hand.

His body deteriorated so quickly after that trip. It was the last time any of us saw him healthy. Hiking. Swimming. . . . But I have no photographic proof, and I will come to deeply regret this during the months that he is dying. I still do. I wish I had video of him jumping in that pool—how he cradled his own body against the cold and said, *Fuck! It's freezing in here!*

I wish I had known to record him singing Scorpions' songs in the car on our way home—his vibrato echoing through the minivan as the kids playfully rolled their eyes, his hands going back and forth between air drums and guitar.

. . . The world is closing in. Did you ever think
That we could be so close, like brothers . . .

That was my favorite Hal. The make-believer. The joker. The charismatic performer. I think it was his favorite Hal, too. Pretending made him feel closer to himself. It was when he seemed happiest. It was when he was the most fun.

Hal and I loved each other most when we were trying to be other people. Masters of pretend. Like every year on Halloween when we went all out, outdoing ourselves in cross-dress extravaganza. It didn't matter if we weren't speaking or how much. When October 31st rolled around, I fell in love with him—as Angela Chase to my Jordan Catalano, Ashley to my Mary-Kate.

One year, we strummed matching guitars as Gunnar and Matthew Nelson. Recorded a faux music video. Tossed our hair back and played our greatest hits.

———

I select random shuffle on the a mixtape I made of all the songs that remind me of Hal, and on the open road, I roll the windows down.

I get lost trying to find the house. There is no signal out here, so my GPS won't work, and without it I'm hopelessly lost. When I think I've finally found the address, I get out and realize I've read the numbers wrong and am actually many miles away.

I circle for more than an hour. Pull over to cry. Get back in my car, scream, keep going. Scream. Finally, I resume service for long enough to screen grab my location and find my way to the house the old-fashioned way—familiarizing myself with my surroundings by way of instinct and voiceless map.

When I finally make it into the house, it is dark as pitch. Desert dark is different from city dark and it occurs to me, as I flick on every possible light in the house that I am scared.

This was a terrible idea, Getting lost was a sign and now I'm stuck here in the middle of nowhere with no GPS. Someone could easily find me, kill me, and no one would know. I guess this is it. I guess I have come here to die.

The desert is hot and dry and wild and dead and yet somehow overwhelmingly alive with howling and flapping and bushes that rustle against the windows. With stars that are so alarmingly bright I can view them with clarity through the window, above my bed.

I will not sleep tonight. I will not sleep tomorrow night, either. I go outside during the day, but do not venture off the property, too afraid I will get lost and be unable to find my way back.

There is no air conditioner, just a swamp cooler, which works in the bedroom but not so much in the main space where I am attempting—and failing—to write. Eventually, I give up trying, realizing that writing is also a crutch. A padding. A way for me to make myself feel less alone. Instead, I'll read a book. I formulate a new set of habits that do not take into consideration anyone but myself. I make single-serve drip coffee over the stove and stop wearing clothes because of the heat. I dance by myself, barefoot in the kitchen with dirty hair. I get acquainted with the property, notice the dozens of empty pans and pots on the periphery and rightly assume they are watering holes. And then I go from pan to ceramic bowl to plastic bucket, filling them up with a watering can.

I talk to Hal out loud, as if he's in the room with me. As if we're once again sharing a bed. I pull memories from the places I have refused to acknowledge until now. How he bought every kind of tampon if I asked him to pick me up a box because he couldn't remember my preferred brand. How excited he got for Christmas mornings, even though he was raised without them. He would happily sit and listen as one of my parents read the kids "Twas the Night Before Christmas." How he would surprise the kids with toys and treats on nights he worked late. And how he always filled our home with the most beautiful music—piano and guitar. And he could sing! You should have heard him sing! Fearlessly, in front of strangers. And everyone loved to be around him at parties. He was always so much fun. Told the best stories. The smartest jokes. How he called me "Leen" and rubbed my feet during all three pregnancies. Told me I was beautiful. Held my hand.

How sometimes he would fall asleep with the kids when he laid down with them and I would have to wake him up. He always did crossword puzzles with a timer, and asked me to check for missed spots when he shaved the back of his head. And then I would slowly work the palm of my hand all the way around his crown, feeling for what I couldn't see.

"Remember that time we ditched marriage counseling and went to lunch instead? How sometimes you would catch me dancing in the kitchen and join me?"

I thought of all of the ways and all the times I had loved him. Even when I didn't want to. I thought of the births of our children and the way his body felt in my arms when he died. I thought of having to pull my car over because I was laughing so hard at something he said. The times I did the same when I was crying. I thought about when we first met, and how I drove home from San Francisco with him on speakerphone, drove straight to his house. How I was so excited to see him, I forgot to lock my car.

The last fight we had, Hal asked me point blank if I wanted a divorce.

"I'll give you one," he had said. "If you can tell me you don't love me anymore."

He had said the same words to me a hundred times before, and every time I shook my head—told him I still loved him—that I would do everything I could to make it work.

This time was different. I was finally done. But more than that, I was finally brave enough to tell him the truth.

"No, I don't love you. Not anymore."

I braced for a reaction but instead he smiled.

"Okay," he said softly. "Then I guess this is it."

He didn't raise his voice. He did the thing that he struggled so hard to do throughout our marriage: he listened to me.

And let me go.

On the third night, I open the sliding glass doors and go outside. I sit down in the chair set up above the property, the one with the best view. I am all alone and I'm still scared but I've done it. After two nights of locking myself in the house, I am now able to stand against the wind in total darkness. Except this time, on my own dare, I invite it in.

This is why I came here. I need to know I can do this part—to hear my voice echo against my own mountaintops across a landscape that isn't buffered by everyone else. To know that life isn't supposed to feel safe and to let it in anyway. Shape-shifting on my own terms. Not unlike like the stars.

Two years ago in the future. Like the picture Revie drew after Hal died. A birthday party in a cemetery, except this one is in the sky.

———

When I was five years old, I was convinced I was part Pegasus. I was so convinced, that when I was alone—when people weren't looking—I quietly whispered to myself in a language all my own. *Pegasaurian* is what I called it, dragging out my hard A's in a whisper. Heyyyyyyyy. It is meiiiiiighhhh agaaaaayyyyyyn.

Unfortunately, and according to what I had convinced myself was Pegasaurian law, the only way for me to grow wings was to do the most embarrassing thing I could think of: get buck naked in the middle of my kindergarten class.

Every day, I went to school with the same plan—to strip down at my desk. To say nothing and swiftly drop trou. Only then would I turn into a flying horse and be *free*.

The closest I came was unbuttoning the top button of my Peter Pan–collared blouse. I cursed myself quietly in my chair. I was a coward. How would I ever become a Pegasus now? I was too afraid. I didn't deserve wings.

As I got older, I often thought of myself in the little orange chair, double dog–daring myself to become a flying animal. I was innocent in those days. Completely sheltered from anything that would suggest I was trying to get attention. I was painfully shy and desperately alone. And in my head, I had convinced myself that the only way out—the only way to become free—was to strip down to nothing. To show the full skin of my Rebeccaness.

In my head, it wouldn't matter what people said about me—I would already be above the clouds. I would never see the likes of any of them again—the humans who never understood. Which is why it wouldn't matter.

But it did, of course. I was always too afraid to be naked in class.

Which is why I stayed a child until I became an adult. There was no shortcut to *being free*. I had chosen to stick it out in my human body, fully clothed.

It took me years to strip down to my bare skin.

Thirty-nine of them. But look now. These words are my wings.

———

When my desert stay is over and it's time for me to go, I do not get lost. All those hours spent going in circles in the wrong direction helped me memorize the mile markers and now I know where to make the right turns toward the highway, no need for GPS.

This is all so familiar now.

My body remembers the curve of the road. It knows that I have been here before. That I have driven past these trees, and crossed that bridge and, *yes, this is where I pulled over to find a signal.*

I may have gotten lost in order to find my way here, but it has helped me find my way home.

Which is where I will go to begin.

Afterword

Hal and I are standing in the middle of an amphitheater on a circle of concrete looking out at a sea of faces. Everyone we've ever known is here and also people we don't. We are waiting for the voices to quiet. I look at Hal for guidance and notice he's clutching a giant book to his chest, like the old photo albums my parents have but ten times as thick. The kind of book you see a small animal holding in a cartoon.

"What is this?" I ask him.

"You'll see," he says.

And then he clears his throat. I don't know how the audience hears him without a microphone, but they do and suddenly all is quiet.

"THANK YOU FOR COMING," he says. "I HAVE SOMETHING TO SHARE WITH YOU."

That's when he opens the book. On the first page is the first photograph we have of each other. My hair is jet black and short, to my ears. He's wearing a purple shirt and a tie. We are sitting at a table together on his thirtieth birthday. The picture is pasted to the book with metallic paper corners you buy from a stationery store.

"Did you make this?" I whisper as he holds the book up to the crowd.

"I did," he says.

I am moved to tears that he did this. That he spent all this time on this book.

"It's taken me months," he says, "but I'm finished now."

The book is bursting with photos, old letters: a scrapbook of our lives together. On the last page is a photo of us that Veronika took the day before Hal died. His eyes are wide, and I am seated beside him on the hospital bed in the oversized sweatshirt our daughter now wears.

I look over at him, confused.

He holds up the last page to the audience and explains, in his own words, that our marriage is over. His words and his story are different than mine because that's how truth works.

"This is the end of us," he says and someone in the crowd—a stranger—raises her hand.

"But why would you end your story now? When there could be so much more?"

"Because," Hal explains, "one of us is dead."

I don't know what he's talking about. That's when he turns to me, tells me it's okay.

"You're alive," he tells me. "You are still alive." He is crying and I am crying, too.

He hands me the book, which I clutch to my chest as I fall down on my knees in front of these people, most of whom I do not know.

And even though our interpretations look different, my truth looks the same in both books. I don't want him to die. But I don't want him to stay, either. I want to wake up to the life I have now. The one without him in it.

And I wonder if they can tell that that's how I feel—these people, friends and strangers, waiting for me to say something meaningful. To tell Hal to *stay with me here, you don't have to die.*

But I can't say those words. Because they aren't true.

Instead I'm on the floor, with the book against my face. The book with all its loose photographs and scrapbook borders around family portraits and road trips and jam sessions and failed birthday parties and burnt toast. And drive-through weddings and car accidents and mortgage liens and matching track suits. And the love two very different people have for their four children.

"Thank you, Hal, for this book," are the last words I say to him before I wake up from my dream. Words I can say because I mean them.

Thank you, Hal, for this book.

Acknowledgments

In middle school, my favorite game to play at sleepovers was *light as a feather, stiff as a board*. It felt like magic to be lifted by so many fingers—many of which belonged to strangers—girls I didn't know who just happened to be at the same slumber party. Some of them loved me and some of them did not but none of them let me go. To this day, I can think of no better metaphor for sisterhood. Feeling lifted in that way, hearing their voices, their stories, underneath my body—trusting them and believing that I was worthy of being carried. That is what it felt like to write this book. So, first, I would like to acknowledge the many humans who by the miracle of fate, ended up at this slumber party, many of whom started as strangers and by morning became friends. Thank you for supporting my work for all of the years I have been writing publicly about my life. Thank you for carrying me on your fingers for the last two decades. You have made me feel safe and seen.

To my agent, Nicki Richesin: you're the real deal and I am so grateful for your grit, fortitude, and the power in which you have stood guard over me and my work.

To my editors and everyone at HarperOne, most notably Hilary Swanson, with whom I shared a first draft that was twice this length(!) and who could not have been more chill when she told me to cut it in half. (She was very right!) You made my book a better book and me a better writer. And to Sydney Rogers for picking up where Hilary left off, seamlessly and with love, faith, and flexibility. Thank you for your patience, advocacy, and care. Endless gratitude to Aidan Mahony, Louise Braverman, and Aly Mostel for your beautiful work.

To my ride or dies, Linda Goldstein Knowlton, April Peveteaux, Jasmine George, Polly Cole, Bethany Winters, Robyn Morrison, Molly Stern, Danielle Hull, Alexa Young, Christina Soletti, Claressinka Anderson, Mindy Laks. I fucking love you all so much. For your words of wisdom, advice, and solidarity, thank you Danielle Henderson, Brook Maurio, and Monique Mitchell. Thank you to Kate Schatz for your brilliance and Jack Murnighan for your insight. And Ashley Van Buren for having all the answers. I love you so much. Thank you Diablo Cody, Roxane Gay, Jenny Lawson, and Lyz Lenz for your willingness to read and blurb so generously. I appreciate you all so much.

Thank you to Jahi Sundance for being my shelter and hype man in the months I was editing and beyond. Your belief in me and love without judgment was and still is a salve. *Like ripples on a blank shore.*

Thank you, Rebecca Coleman and Chelsea Gilmore for telling me I would write this book before I even knew that I could. I love you both more than you will ever know.

Thank you to Veronika Shulman for a friendship that has expanded and redefined for me what it means to be a life partner. Thank you for feeding me in every possible way. Life really is better with a Giant Schnauzer. I love you forever.

Thank you to Erica Tanamachi—my sister-cousin. You came to me and never left. You always have.

And to Monica Danielle, thank you for opening me up to a different and wholly expansive kind of love—for reading every draft and pushing me forward—for knowing me in a way no one has before.

Thank you to all names-have-been-changed lovers who will never read this book and also those who will. Sometimes *the king is a woman* and sometimes the muse is a man. And to those who read this book and realized they couldn't love me afterwards, thank you for reminding me that a love without truth isn't love.

I wrote the entirety of this book on my unmade bed, surrounded by laundry while quarantining with four children. It was noisy and intense and there was absolutely no peace to be found but I did the work anyway. Just like women have always done. So I would like to thank the chaos—of which I have become so accustomed to all these years —for keeping me humble and honest and for humanizing my experience. Life is loud and messy and full of noises we cannot control. Learning how to work under those circumstances, I think, has made me a better writer. Certainly, a more patient one.

For my family and extended family—my dad, the greatest man, father and grandfather to exist—thank you for loving and supporting me unconditionally and for calling me out *only* on typos. To my brilliant siblings, Rachel, David, and Alyssa, and my grandmothers, Betty and Pat: you have only ever loved me without judgment and rooted me on. I am so lucky to be yours.

To Susan. For loving, supporting, and holding space for me, even when it's complicated, thank you. I love you completely.

For Archer, Fable, Bo, and Revie—my babies, friends, the loves of my life. Thank you for trusting me and asking me hard questions. Thank you for dancing with me in the kitchen between chapters. You are the four points of my compass and the whole of my heart.

And lastly, to my mother, who fortified every page of this book with her eyes and heart and willingness to open up to me in ways that made me feel seen as only she could. Because of her honesty and guidance both personally and editorially, I was better able to understand myself—not as the daughter, the mother, or the wife, but as the woman, the writer.

Mom—your belief in me since girlhood has made me brave. I was able to write this book because of you.

About the Author

REBECCA WOOLF is an award-winning writer and blogger who has been featured in outlets such as the *New York Times*, *TIME* magazine, and NPR. She lives in LA with her four children.

Instagram: rebeccawooolf
Twitter: @GirlsGoneChild
Website: rebeccawoolf.com